TRAVERSE
THEATRE

**TRAVERSE THEATRE and PETER WOLFF THEATRE TRUST
present TRAVERSE THEATRE COMPANY**

PERFECT DAYS

A Romantic Comedy
by Liz Lochhead

cast in order of appearance

Barbs Marshall	Siobhan Redmond
Alice Inglis	Anne Kidd
Sadie Kirkwood	Ann Scott-Jones
Brendan Boyle	John Kazek
Davie Marshall	Vincent Friell
Grant Steel	Enzo Cilenti

directed by	John Tiffany
designed by	Georgia Sion
lighting designed by	Chahine Yavroyan
sound designed by	John Harris
re-lights	Maria-Theresa Bechaalani
stage manager	Nils den Hertog
deputy stage manager	Patricia Kenny
assistant stage manager	Mike Fitton
wardrobe supervisor	Lynn Ferguson
wardrobe assistant	Alice Taylor

First performed at the Traverse Theatre Friday 7 August 1998;
first performance of this revival 6 January 1999
at Hampstead Theatre, London.

TRAVERSE THEATRE

One of the most important theatres in Britain The Observer

Edinburgh's **Traverse Theatre** is Scotland's new writing theatre, with a 35 year record of excellence. With quality, award-winning productions and programming, the Traverse receives accolades at home and abroad from audiences and critics alike.

The Traverse has an unrivalled reputation for producing contemporary theatre of the highest quality, invention and energy, commissioning and supporting writers from Scotland and around the world and facilitating numerous script development workshops, rehearsed readings and public writing workshops. The Traverse aims to produce several major new theatre productions plus a Scottish touring production each year. It is unique in Scotland in its exclusive dedication to new writing, providing the infrastructure, professional support and expertise to ensure the development of a sustainable and relevant theatre culture for Scotland and the UK.

Traverse Theatre Company productions have been seen worldwide including in London, Toronto, Budapest and New York. Recent touring successes in Britain include PASSING PLACES by Stephen Greenhorn, HERITAGE by Nicola McCartney and LAZYBED by Iain Crichton Smith.

The Traverse can be relied upon to produce more
good-quality new plays than any other Fringe venue
Daily Telegraph

During the Edinburgh Festival the Traverse is one of the most important venues with world class premieres playing daily in the two theatre spaces. The Traverse won *ten* awards at the 1998 Edinburgh Festival Fringe, including *Scotsman Fringe Firsts* for Traverse productions KILL THE OLD TORTURE THEIR YOUNG by David Harrower and PERFECT DAYS by Liz Lochhead.

An essential element of the Traverse Company's activities takes place within the educational sector, concentrating on the process of playwriting for young people. The Traverse flagship education project BANK OF SCOTLAND CLASS ACT offers young people in schools the opportunity to work with theatre professionals and see their work performed on the Traverse stage. In addition the Traverse Young Writers group, led by professional playwrights, has been running for almost three years and meets weekly.

LIZ LOCHHEAD

Liz Lochhead's stage plays include *Britannia Rules, Mary Queen of Scots got her Head Chopped Off, Quelques Fleurs, Shanghaied, The Big Picture* and *Cuba*, as well as acclaimed adaptations of, among others, Bram Stoker's *Dracula*, Molière's *Tartuffe* and *The York Mystery Plays*. PERFECT DAYS was her first commission for the Traverse since *Blood and Ice* in 1982.

FOREWORD

Heartfelt thanks are due to several friends:

Willie Russell asked me something a few years ago which really made me think. This wasn't the question he asked me, but I began to wonder whether I could write something for the stage with a happy ending...

It's a while ago now, but Marilyn Imrie, Pamela Wilson, Joe Ahearne and Bill Forsyth read a short script of mine, an episide one or a first act, about a modern Glasgow girl, a bit of an entrepreneurial genius, a hairdresser who, pushing forty, finds herself with a biologically imperative, if emotionally and sexually rather inconvenient, now-or-never desire to have a baby. They were all very encouraging indeed - Bill, in one of those 'You could do this, you could do that' conversations, casually suggested something which became absolutely fundamental to the plot and for which I am *very* grateful - but mainly they all made me realise it was a story I really wanted to write. And while I could, in those early days, decide to try and tell it for radio, for television and for film, I certainly wanted to tell it as a single drama. A story that would end once my heroine's pursuit was finally played out and she either got,or realised she would never get, her Heart's Desire. Soon I knew that I wanted to write my favourite kind of film, the romantic comedy, in the form of a single set stage play.

Two scenes and a conversation were enough to convince Philip Howard and, hurrah, he commissioned it. My gratitude to him, and to the soon-on-board John Tiffany, at the Traverse - both of whom have pushed the script all the way - is boundlesss.

Iain Heggie and Colin Chambers both read the first draft and made extensive written notes for me which resulted in both fundamental structural changes and inumerable, but vital, tweaks.

I wrote the part of Barbs Marshall with Siobhan Redmond's voice, self and laugh always in my mind. Her early commitment to the project made it happen. This play is for Siobhan with love and thanks.

Liz Lochhead July 1998

BIOGRAPHIES
in alphabetical order

ENZO CILENTI *(Grant Steel)*: Trained: Drama Studio, London. Productions whilst training include: BOUND AND TRUST, AN ABSOLUTE TURKEY, THE COUNTRY WIFE, THE WAY OF THE WORLD, OTHELLO, LOVE'S LABOURS LOST, ROMEO AND JULIET, A WINTER'S TALE, THE THREE SISTERS, ARCADIA and DEALING WITH CLAIR. Television work includes: COPS, TRIAL AND RETRIBUTION 2, FOOLSDAY and A DANCE TO THE MUSIC OF TIME.

VINCENT FRIELL *(Davie Marshall)*: Born and educated in Glasgow. For the Traverse: PERFECT DAYS (Festival 98), TALLY'S BLOOD. Other theatre work includes: IN TIME OF STRIFE (7:84); THE LUCKY ONES, THE TEMPEST (TAG); SLAB BOYS TRILOGY (Dundee Rep); THE PRIME OF MISS JEAN BRODIE (Brunton); MR GILLIE (Scottish Theatre Co.); DANTON'S DEATH (Communicado); AMERICAN BUFFALO (Winged Horse); WALTER (EIF); HARD TIMES, UNCLE VANYA, WHITE BIRD PASSES (Dundee Rep); THE HOUSE AMONG THE STARS (Perth Rep); SLAB BOYS TRILOGY (Young Vic); ARSENIC AND OLD LACE (Arches); NO EXPENSE SPARED (Wildcat); A WHOLLY HEALTHY GLASGOW (Dressing Room); SABINA (Borderline); DON JUAN (Theatre Highland). Television work includes: TAGGART, WOMAN AT WAR, HIGH ROAD (STV); END OF THE LINE, KNOCKBACK, RAB C NESBITT, PARAHANDY (BBC); COUNTRY DIARY OF AN EDWARDIAN LADY (Granada); ROUGHNECKS (First Choice). Film includes: TRAINSPOTTING, RESTLESS NATIVES.

JOHN HARRIS (sound designer): For the Traverse: ANNA WEISS, KNIVES IN HENS, GRETA, SHARP SHORTS. Other theatre work includes: STOCKAREE, OF NETTLES AND ROSES (Theatre Workshop); NOT FOR THE FANFARE (First Base); THE NEST, M'LADY MALADE, THE GREAT THEATRE OF THE WORLD, MANKIND, THE TEMPEST (True Belleek); THE ELVES AND THE SHOEMAKER (Reppe). Musical Direction includes: MASS (Bernstein); AFRICAN SANCTUS (Fanshawe); CARMINA BURANA (Orff); HIAWATHA (Bogdanov). John is also commissioned as a classical composer and works as assistant organist at St Giles' Cathedral, Edinburgh.

JOHN KAZEK *(Brendan Boyle)*: For the Traverse: PASSING PLACES, THE CHIC NERDS, STONES AND ASHES, EUROPE. Other theatre work includes: MACBETH, A DOLL'S HOUSE (Theatre Babel); MARABOU STORK NIGHTMARES (Citizens', Leicester Haymarket); MARY QUEEN OF SCOTS GOT HER HEAD CHOPPED OFF, KIDNAPPED, CARLUCCO AND THE QUEEN OF HEARTS (Lyceum); DIAL M FOR MURDER (Dundee Rep); LOOT, DRIVING MISS DAISY, CAN'T PAY, WON'T PAY (Byre); ORPHANS (Harbinger); NAE PROBLEM, GOVAN STORIES, JUMP THE LIFE TO COME (7:84); AS YOU LIKE IT, KING LEAR (Oxford Stage Co); GREAT EXPECTATIONS (Lyric, Belfast); JUST FRANK (Theatre Royal, Stratford East). Television and film work includes: RAB C NESBITT, PUNCH DRUNK, DOUBLE NOUGAT, NERVOUS ENERGY, STRATHBLAIR (BBC); ALBERT AND THE LION (STV); SILENT SCREAM (Antonine Productions); RIFF RAFF (Parallax Pictures).

ANNE KIDD *(Alice Inglis)*: For the Traverse: PERFECT DAYS (Festival 98), WIDOWS. Theatre work includes: BORN GUILTY, CALEDONIA DREAMING, ANGELS IN AMERICA (7:84); THE GRAPES OF WRATH (7:84/Dundee Rep); THE SNOW QUEEN (MacRobert Arts Centre); SCOTS QUAIR (TAG); THE PRICE (Royal Lyceum); SPIDER'S WEB, THE NORMAN CONQUESTS (Pitlochry Festival Theatre); THE DEEP BLUE SEA, MY COUSIN RACHEL, ONE FLEW OVER THE CUCKOO'S NEST (Perth Rep); THE RISING OF THE MOON (Old Red Lion); RELATIVELY SPEAKING (Watermill); AGNES OF GOD (Belgrade Studio, Coventry); DUET FOR ONE (Birmingham Rep); MOTHER COURAGE, THE MATCHMAKER, BRAND, LOVES LABOURS LOST (Nottingham Playhouse); ANDROCLES AND THE LION (Regent's Park Open Air); WHAT EVERY WOMAN KNOWS (Brunton); OLD TIMES (Exeter). Television includes: DOCTOR FINLAY, TAGGART (STV); THE CYCLIST, TUTTI FRUTTI, THE LOVE SCHOOL, THE GHOST SONATA, SUTHERLAND'S LAW, ANGLES, KING ARTHUR (BBC). Film includes: PORT OF SECRETS, GREGORY'S TWO GIRLS.

SIOBHAN REDMOND *(Barbs Marshall)*: For the Traverse: SHADOWING THE CONQUEROR. Other theatre work includes: SPANISH TRAGEDY, MUCH ADO ABOUT NOTHING (RSC); AN EXPERIENCED WOMAN GIVES ADVICE (Manchester Royal Exchange); THE TRICK IS TO KEEP BREATHING (Tron/Toronto/Royal Court); SEX COMEDIES (Touring); THE DREAM, KING LEAR, LOOK BACK IN ANGER (Renaissance); CARMEN (Communicado); AS YOU LIKE IT (Royal Lyceum); THE BIG PICTURE (Dundee Rep); GOLDILOCKS (Grand Opera House, Belfast); A MONTH OF SUNDAYS (Nuffield/Duchess); MACBETH (Tron); DON JUAN THE LOVER (Crucible Sheffield). Television work includes: IN THE RED, NERVOUS ENERGY, CAPTIVE, BETWEEN THE LINES, THE HIGH LIFE, SORRY ABOUT LAST NIGHT, THE DUNROMAN RISING, CASUALTY, RIDES, RELATIVE STRANGER, THE HIGH LIFE, RAB C NESBITT, END OF THE LINE, SWEET NOTHINGS (BBC); WOKENWELL (LWT); THROWAWAYS (Zenith); DEACON BRODIE (Tiger Aspect); HARD CASES (Central); LOOK BACK IN ANGER (Renaissance); THE BILL, TEA BAGS (Thames); DAD ON ARRIVAL (STV/Channel 4); TAGGART (STV); CORDING, GRAVY TRAIN, AT THE END OF ALEX (Portman Productions); BULMAN, ALFRESCO, NOTHING TO WORRY ABOUT (Granada). Film work includes: BEAUTIFUL PEOPLE (Beautiful Stories Ltd); KARMIC MOTHERS (BBC Tartan Short); DUET FOR ONE.

ANN SCOTT JONES *(Sadie Kirkwood)*: For the Traverse: LAZYBED. Other theatre work includes: THE BIG PICTURE by Liz Lochhead (Dundee Rep); RED HOT SHOES, THE MARBLE MADONNA, THE GUID SISTERS (Tron); THE GLASS MENAGERIE, SHINDA THE MAGIC APE (Royal Lyceum); PRECARIOUS LIVING, THE GIN GAME, BRIGHTON BEACH MEMOIRS, STEEL MAGNOLIAS, GASLIGHT, THE MATING GAME (Perth Rep); WITNESS FOR THE PROSECUTION, A FLEA IN HER EAR, ALL MY SONS, THE STEAMIE, DEAR BRUTUS, CAUSE CELEBRE (Pitlochry). Television includes: THE NUCLEAR FAMILY, IT COULD HAPPEN TO ANYBODY, EDGE OF DARKNESS, LET'S SEE, JUTE CITY, BREAKING THE ANGELS BACK, A LIFE IN CHINA, STRATHBLAIR, THE CELTS, THE HIGH LIFE (BBC); THE PRINCESS STALLION, HIGH ROAD, THE PERSONAL TOUCH (STV); JOHN BROWN'S BODY, CLASSIC CHILDREN'S TALES, MILES BETTER (Channel 4). Film work includes: RESTLESS NATIVES, LOCAL HERO, GREYSTOKE, SOFT TOP, HARD SHOULDER, AN ANGEL PASSES BY. Ann has worked extensively in radio, most recently the Woman's Hour serial STILL WATERS and Christmas Day's STORYLINE.

GEORGIA SION (designer): Theatre work includes: LOVERS (RSC Fringe Festival); SLEEPING AROUND (Paines Plough); CUT AND RUNNING (Battersea Arts Centre); RICHARD III (Arts Threshold); SHIFT (Old Red Lion); THE SUNSET SHIP (Young Vic Theatre Company); OTHELLO (Watermill Theatre/Tokyo Globe); TWELFTH NIGHT (Central School of Speech and Drama); THE WEAVERS (The Gate); AFORE NIGHT COME (Theatr Clwyd). Opera includes: A-RONNE, A MEDICINE FOR MELANCHOLY (ENO Baylis Program); KING AND MARSHAL (Bloomsbury Theatre); FOUR SAINTS IN THREE ACTS (Trinity Opera).

JOHN TIFFANY (director): Trained: Glasgow University. Literary Director at the Traverse since June 1997. He directed GRETA, PASSING PLACES (97 & 98), SHARP SHORTS and co-directed STONES AND ASHES for the Traverse. Other theatre includes: HIDE AND SEEK and BABY, EAT UP (LookOut); THE SUNSET SHIP (Young Vic); GRIMM TALES (Leicester Haymarket); EARTHQUAKE WEATHER (Starving Artists). Film includes: KARMIC MOTHERS (BBC Tartan Shorts) and GOLDEN WEDDING (BBC Two Lives).

CHAHINE YAVROYAN (lighting designer): Trained: Bristol Old Vic Theatre School. For the Traverse: PERFECT DAYS (Festival 98), KILL THE OLD TORTURE THEIR YOUNG, ANNA WEISS, KNIVES IN HENS, THE ARCHITECT, SHINING SOULS. Other theatre work includes: HEDDA GABLER, WOLK'S WORLD (Manchester Royal Exchange); VILLETTE, KING LEAR, SOUTH PACIFIC (Crucible); ONE MORE WASTED YEAR, BAZAAR, A STRANGERS HOUSE (Royal Court at The Ambassadors); SHANG-A-LANG (Bush); VARIETE (Lindsay Kemp); TANTAMOUNT ESPERANCE (Rose English); UBU KUNST (Platform 2); LA MUSICA DEUXIEME, GAUCHO (Hampstead). Dance work includes: FORREST DANCERS No 1-4 (Bock & Vincenzi); BLIND FAITH (Yolande Snaith Theatredance); HEART/HOME, GALLIARD (Rosie Lee). Site specific work includes: DREAMWORK (LWT Youth Challenge); SNAKES AND LADDERS, SALISBURY TALES (Station House Opera, Salisbury); HAUGHMOND DANCES, ASCENDING FIELDS (Rosie Lee); HOUSES, TALES FROM THE CITY (Geraldine Pilgrim); ECCLECT DISSECT, PARIS, TEXAS (Givenchy) and various events and celebrations for the city of Bologna, Italy.

PERFECT DAYS

props & costumes created by Traverse workshops
funded by the National Lottery

Traverse computer systems funded by the National Lottery

for PERFECT DAYS:

Set built by Pitlochry Festoval Theatre

Production Photography Kevin Low

Print Photography Euan Myles

Additional work on costumes Jackie Holt

**For generous help with PERFECT DAYS
the Traverse Theatre thanks:**

HABITAT, Edinburgh ● STRAND LIGHTING ● Frasers, Edinburgh
Flower Factory ● Rock Sensations ● Salon Services ● W.T. Dunbar & Sons
Edinburgh Architectural Salvage Yard
Cheynes Hairdressing (Also: Jack, Cheynes Hair Stylist)
Penny Kennedy Design ● Electra Com ● P.U. Components, Halifax
Hanson White Cards ● Round The World Aya Kobayashi
Traverse Bar Café ● James Ritchie, Edinburgh
Start Rite Shoes ● Oddbins, Bruntsfield ● Citizens' Theatre, Glasgow
Royal Lyceum Theatre, Edinburgh ● National Galleries Of Scotland
Waterstones, Eastend, Edinburgh ● D.C Thompson, Dundee
Hello Magazine, London ● Hammersmith & Fulham Libraries, London
Mothercare, Edinburgh ● Hilly Cat Jones ● Anna Lau ● Liz Lochhead
LEVER BROTHERS for Wardrobe Care ● BLF

The spring 1999 tour of PERFECT DAYS will be seen at the
Kings Theatre (Edinburgh), His Majesty's Theatre (Aberdeen), and Eden Court
(Inverness). These theatres along with the Kings Theatre and Theatre Royal
(Glasgow) and Festival Theatre (Edinburgh) have been working together to
ensure that large scale productions are seen throughout Scotland.

TRAVERSE THEATRE • THE COMPANY

Maria-Theresa Bechaalani
Deputy Electrician

Stephen Bremner
Deputy Bar Manager

Nils den Hertog
Stage Manager

Calum Chaplin
Head Chef

Janet Dick
Cleaner

Lynn Ferguson
Wardrobe Supervisor

Mike Fitton
Assistant Stage Manager

Jean Fitzsimons
Box Office Manager

Michael Fraser
Theatre Manager

Gary Glen
Café Supervisor

Mike Griffiths
Production Manager

Paul Hackett
Finance Manager

Noelle Henderson
Development Manager

Jamie Higgins
2nd Chef

Philip Howard
Artistic Director

Ruth Kent
Assistant Box Office Manager

Mark Leese
Design Associate

Yvonne McDevitt
Assistant Director

Niall Macdonald
Bar Manager

Catherine MacNeil
Assistant Administrator

Jan McTaggart
Marketing & Press Officer

Lucy Mason
Administrative Producer

Lorraine May
Front of House Manager

David Moore
Assistant Accountant

Brian Mundie
Marketing/Box Office Asst

Duncan Nicoll
Assistant Bar Manager

Victoria Paulo
Deputy Stage Manager

Catherine Robertson
Administrative Assistant

Renny Robertson
Chief Electrician

Angelo Rodrigues
Kitchen Assistant

Hannah Rye
Literary Assistant

Fiona Sturgeon
Marketing Manager

Richard Stembridge
Production Assistant

Alice Taylor
Wardobe Assistant

John Tiffany
Literary Director

Ella Wildridge
Literary Associate

ALSO WORKING FOR THE TRAVERSE
Mercedes Alcon Camas, Lesley Alyward, Felix Balfour, Sarah Louise Bowman, Anna Copland, Andrew Coyle, Robert Evans, Ben Ewart-Dean, Hilary Galloway, Nicola Glasgow, Linda Gunn, David Henderson, Malcolm Hamilton, Marigold Hope, David Inverarity, Katherine Johnston, Louise Kemp, Linda Keys, Craig Kincaid, Marie Kotz, Sophie Logan, Graeme Maley, Nadine Mery, Graziano Pozzi, Rowan Risby, Sarah Shiel, Ben Thomson, Carolina Van Wyk, Lucy Walsh, Matthew Wellard, Nicole Wise

TRAVERSE THEATRE - BOARD OF DIRECTORS
John Scott Moncrieff, Chair, **Sir Eddie Kulukundis OBE**, Vice President **Stuart Hepburn**, Vice Chair, **Scott Howard**, Secretary **Kate Atkinson, Barry Ayre, Geraldine Gammell, Lesley Riddoch**

SPONSORSHIP

Sponsorship income enables the Traverse to commission and produce new plays and offer audiences a diverse and exciting programme of events throughout the year.

We would like to thank the following companies for their support throughout the year.

⚛ BANK OF SCOTLAND

CORPORATE ASSOCIATE SCHEME

LEVEL ONE

Balfour Beatty
Scottish Life the PENSION company
United Distillers & Vintners

LEVEL TWO
Laurence Smith &Son
- *Wine and Spirit Merchants*
NB Information
Willis Corroon Scotland Ltd

LEVEL THREE
Alistir Tait FGA
- *Antiques & Fine Jewellery*
Allingham & Co, Solicitors
Nicholas Groves Raines
Architects
KPMG
Scottish Post Office Board
The McCabe Partnership
Chartered Accountants

With thanks to
Navy Blue Design, print designers for the Traverse
and to George Stewarts the printers.
Purchase of the Traverse Box Office and computer network has been made possible with funds from the National Lottery.

The Traverse Theatre's work would not be possible without the support of

THE SCOTTISH ARTS COUNCIL   ·EDINBVRGH·
THE CITY OF EDINBURGH COUNCIL

The Traverse receives financial assistance for its educational and development work from
John Lewis Partnership, Save and Prosper Charitable Trusts, Binks Trust, The Bulldog Prinsep Theatrical Fund, Calouste Gulbenkian Foundation

Charity No. SC002368

PERFECT DAYS

a romantic comedy

Characters

BARBS MARSHALL, 39, *a Glasgow celebrity hairdresser*

ALICE INGLIS, 44, *Barbs's oldest friend*

SADIE KIRKWOOD, 62, *Barbs's mother*

BRENDAN BOYLE, 27-37, *Barbs's best friend*

DAVIE MARSHALL 42, *Barbs's estranged husband*

GRANT STEEL, 26, *an attractive stranger*

The action of this play is all set in the same large and very stylish Merchant City Loft in Glasgow, Barbs Marshall's home.

The scenes take place consecutively on nine different days in Barbs's life. They span from Scene One, a week or so before her thirty-ninth birthday, till Scene Ten, about eighteen months later.

ACT ONE

Scene One

*Music – it's Dusty Springfield singing 'I'm Going Back' (and it's
the second verse ending ' . . . Now there's more to do than watch
my sailboat glide / And every day can be my magic carpet ride /
And I can play hide and seek with my fears / And live my days
instead of counting my years.') Fades out as the lights go up.*

ALICE INGLIS, *a handsome and pleasant looking woman in her
early forties, sits in her clean M&S slip on a chair in the middle
of this large space. A trendy loft. (to one side, off, is the kitchen, to
the other, off, bathroom / bedroom. There is a loft bed or
mezzanine above part of this living-space. Centre back, there is a
large door into the public hallway, the outside world.*

BARBS MARSHALL, *a very flamboyantly attractive woman in
her late thirties is just finishing cutting* ALICE*'s hair. The last two
snips and she picks up the newspaper on which the fall of
clippings is caught and pours it into the waste bin.*

*Around them, piled on the sofa, are some expensive and chic
clothes.*

BARBS. So, Alice, I was telling you, we get to Glasgow airport,
guy on the desk recognises me, we get an upgrade, very nice,
thank you very much, First Class practically empty, great,
spread out a bit, relax, the champagne cocktails, the blue blue
sky, the white fluffy clouds beneath us . . . I'm feeling: OK
maybe he's not got the highest IQ in the world but he does
have a gorgeous profile and at least he's not wearing that
fucking awful jumper that he turned up in wan night, tucked
into his trousers can you believe, and gave me a red neck in
front of Brendan from work.

I mean true and everlasting love it is not, but he's a nice guy
and all that, own teeth, daft about me, well so far, it's only
been three or four weeks, defin-ately dead keen, or so I've been
led to believe by the dinners, the phonecalls, the nipping my
heid about Paris – how he used to live there how there are all

these sweet wee dinky little special places he knows that he'd like to take me, so there we are, we get to the hotel and here they've overbooked so this time we get an automatic upgrade to the four star no problem, it's gorgeous, the corner room, the fruitbowl, the flowers, the complimentary chocolates, the half bottle of champagne, the big kingsize bed all turned down at the corner . . . And – now, to let you know, Alice – back home in Glasgow I've been avoiding it, by the way, because truth to tell I do not really fancy him, at least I do not fancy him when I am actually *with* him, I've been, frankly, postponing the inevitable for this weekend where I have calculated, quite correctly according to my Predictor Kit, I will be *ovulating* – and he says to me he can't sleep with me because he's Met Someone and he's fallen in love! No, correction, he can *sleep* with me, but we can't have sex because that would be him being unfaithful to his new wee dolly inamorata.

I'm like: What? I'm like: What are we doing here? And Why? He's like: well, it's a fantastic city, and I'm his best friend – best friend! – and he wants to show me it and he didn't want to disappoint me!

Chin*ese*!

ALICE. Men! Eh? What a fucking wanker!

BARBS. I'm like . . . naah, he won't be able to last out, *but* we go for dinner, we walk along the Seine in the moonlight, we have a couple of brandies, and yet, no, quite oblivious to me and all my brand new extortionate La Perla flimsies bought special, nope – bedtime, he pecks me chastely on the cheek and falls fast and instantly asleep, snoring away like billyo while I am lying there wide awake and just bloody raging.

Because, apart from the galling fact that one of my dwindling supply of eggs is up there, yet again going to waste for want of the Sparky Sperm the Tadpole with its name on it, now that I can't have him do I not start to fancy him something chronic? Torture.

ALICE. Mental!

BARBS. So much for the Romantic fucking Winterbreak Valentine Special Weekend in Paris. I mean you lower your standards to minus zero, decide you'll settle for fuck all and even that is denied one.

ALICE *laughs.* BARBS *is taken aback then joins in.*

BARBS. Well I guess I'll always have Paris . . . (*Beat.*) Product!

BARBS *applies a scoosh of mousse to* ALICE*'s hair.*

ALICE. Barbs, this is helluva good of you pal, but don't go to a lot of bother.

BARBS. Nearly done . . . Wur Own Make. Softstyle shinegel megamousse. This is *the* styling product out of the range that may well yet bankrupt Razor City. However, Stefan would not be deflected from his dreams, would he? And I do have to admit it is a super product. Among a market chocabloc jampacked hoaching with super products . . .

Don't move.

ALICE. Ach, as long as I'm neat and tidy . . .

BARBS. Alice, you get your hair cut. By me. At my home. Which is something I have never done for *anybody* since 1978 –

ALICE. I'm sorry, I'm sorry, I know, I know, I didny mean it like that . . . yes, I'm an ungrateful bitch, so I am. I know. I mean, here am urr getting styled by The Stylist that every single person on Morningtime Makeover fights over –

BARBS. Exactly. Doing your hair for you in the privacy of her own home so that tonight you will look *fabulous.* Neat and tidy your arse Alice!

So – Paris – you'd think that was bad enough. That was me. Hu-miliated. Following month I'm like forget it. Month after that same. Then the next month, unexpectedly, something presents itself . . .

ALICE. Barbs, excuse me, but can you not get that artificial insemination stuff?

BARBS. Yes, Alice, you can, but something about it does not appeal to me. Maybe I do not like to think of having to tell my baby its daddy is a wanker . . .

They both laugh.

BARBS. Na, for some reason . . . Maybe it's aesthetic, maybe it's pride . . .

ALICE. You could always go back to our Davie!

BARBS. Aye right!

ALICE. He's crazy about you, Barbs, he's never ever got over you.

BARBS. Aye right, aye! *Anyway* Howard next door –

ALICE. The dishy one?

BARBS. P.G.L.

ALICE. Eh?

BARBS. Pointless good looks . . . Computers. Anyway, he's always been after me. My Midnight Caller. He wished. But I've always knocked him back. Well, obviously he's never come out with it in so many words, it's just been a matter of my not taking him on, never giving him any encouragement, nipping it in the bud sort of thing, you know what I mean?

ALICE. No really.

BARBS. *Aye* you do. Well turns out Howard is moving out, going to Singapore on a three year contract, has sold the loft, this is him in for a nightcap saying cheeritata for ever, one thing leads to another, I realise it's Mid Cycle . . . *As* you say Howard is nice looking, is obviously highly intelligent, good bet genetically, I mean the missing bits I can put down to bad conditioning which no way would I be guilty of, and best of all he is leaving. For good. Well, one thing leads to yet another, I tell him no need for precautions I've got a coil, which is a lie but he doesn't know that, he says it's OK anyway because before he left his marriage he got an eternity ring vasectomy!

ALICE. A what?

BARBS. Common phenomenon. Big article about it in the Marie Claire. Middle-aged marriage begins to show cracks, man has affair, wife finds out, goes mental, threatens suicide or that he'll never see the kids again, husband shits himself, dumps dollybird, promises wife never again, very sorry, totally into marriage and this family *and*, to demonstrate one hundred and ten percent commitment to the status quo, from now on *he* will do the contraception and Have Vasectomy as family teenage and complete. But nevertheless marriage breaks down anyway as fucked, basically, inevitable, and ends up with man in new relationship with much younger woman who is deprived of her own children because his vasectomy turns out to be irreversible.

ALICE. What happens to the wife?

BARBS. How do I know what happens to the wife? She moves to the Borders with her new partner, a much younger man who is a furniture maker or something, I don't fucking know.

ALICE. You'd think they'd tell you what happens to the wife.

BARBS. Listen, Alice, the article was in the Marie Claire not the bloody Good Housekeeping, OK?

ALICE. I didn't know Howard was married before.

BARBS. Howard's been married, he's lived with the younger woman, been dumped by her, and now he's fucked off forever to Singapore without doing me the very small favour which it seems it's too much to ask for these days.

Plus the sex was terrible.

I mean to me, well I guess I'm just a pure product of my generation, but to me sex is about sex. Sometimes, when you are lucky, sex is about love. But sex as anything to do with pregnancy? Humping Howard was my idea of nothing to do, quite frankly.

Mibbe I'll end up at the artificial insemination clinic yet.

Only it seems so . . . clinical . . .

Maybe I could *pay* somebody . . .

ALICE. Make it somebody gorgeous well!

BARBS. Naturally. A big cock and a high I.Q. Anyway, Alice, I've told *you* everything, so tell. Tell. Who was he?

ALICE. Who?

BARBS. You know who. Gorgeous that you were having your lunch with in thon place in Princes Square. I saw you.

Shutters come down in ALICE. *She's clearly very taken aback.*

ALICE. I never saw you.

BARBS. Too right you never saw me. I was going to come over. I *approached*, I was coming over when just something about the two of you made me go . . . *naaa.*

ALICE. It was a meeting.

BARBS. How old was he anyway?

ALICE. It was a work thing.

BARBS. Nice work if you can get it. Tell!

ALICE. There's nothing to tell . . .

BARBS. Nothing to tell you are sat there the middle of the day
the middle of the week looking fabulous, honestly you were
like a girl, Alice, the *glow,* the animation, like a *lover*, do I
know love when I see it? I think *so,* I could see the lovelight in
your eyes, sat there, Alice, with the dolliest Toyboy in the West
sitting there opposite you hanging on your every word,
drinking you in? What is going on?

BARBS *stares at* ALICE *sure she'll tell.* ALICE *stares back,
sure she's not going to. A beat. Finally –*

ALICE. Barbs . . .

BARBS. Alice!

ALICE. Listen Barbs, you didn't need to go to all this bother.

BARBS. That's right, change the Subject!

ALICE. Barbs, how long have you known me?

BARBS. Just about all my life.

ALICE. And how long have I been married to Tommy?

BARBS. Donkeys . . .

ALICE. Twenty-two year come November.

BARBS. You're kidding! Christ, I'd hotpants on. Davie and I had
only been going wi each other about a month or something, he
wasny allowed to bring us to the meal, I was only invited to the
reception . . . Twenty-tw –

ALICE. Twenty-two years. Tommy and I. And do I strike you as
the toyboy type?

BARBS. No. I can't say that has been my impression. Up till now.

ALICE. Well, then.

BARBS. How is Tommy?

ALICE. He's fine.

BARBS. And the girls?

ALICE. Thank God. Wee Andrea's got her Highers this year, so we'll just have to see how she gets on. Our Noelene could knock spots off her in the studying department . . .

BARBS. Give them my love.

ALICE. Course I will.

BARBS. Gorgeous kids you've got.

ALICE. They're all right. They're nice girls, I suppose. Touch wood.

Barbs, see this having a baby idea that you've suddenly come out with, out the blue . . . ?

BARBS. Out the blue nothing, Alice! Doesn't every woman want a pop at pregnancy before her womb goes pearshape?

ALICE. I've never ever seen you as the wanting kids type. In fact, haven't you always worked very hard to make sure that this was never ever the option? I mean if you'd wanted kids would you have split up with our Davie and put Heart Soul and Hormones into Razor City and your telly career?

Do you no think you've mibbe got romantic ideas – from where I don't know! – in your head about it all? Motherhood . . .

I mean it's hard work, they're not a toy –

BARBS. I know it's bloody hard work, Alice!

ALICE. But darlin' you *don't* know.

BARBS. Don't you fucking dare mention this to anybody whatsoever!

ALICE. I won't. I wouldn't! Course not . . . Barbs, I'm sorry, listen, it's none of my business –

BARBS. It isn't.

ALICE. This is helluva good of you, pal, I mean I only phoned up for some advice about what to wear and that, I didn't – honestly – expect my own personal makeover.

I'd of thought you'd be busy anyway, the weekend and that . . .

BARBS. Aye I'd to cancel three dinnerparties and a film premiere.

ALICE. It's only a daft work thing.

BARBS. At which you are going to look fan-fucking-tastic.

ALICE. For the Gartsheuch Housing Association executive
committee and the deputy director of Scottish Homes?

BARBS. You won your lottery funding for your centre didn't you?
So tonight you are going to look A Million Dollars. Anyway,
I'm about done. Let me show you the back . . .

ALICE. That's neat. That's nice and neat into the back of the neck
anyway.

BARBS. *Neat?* It's *fab*ulous. How I want you to do it yourself,
you need product, that's *essential*, but not too much right, I'll
give you this away with you, just lift with the heel of your
hand, roughen it up, just to give rootlift, then either a touch of
wax, or – better – the totiest drop of freeze and shine rubbed
on your fingertips, then – Alice are you actually listening to
me? – see, I've just *chipped* into your fringe –

ALICE. Well, that'll go wi the *mug* underneath it! Haw, haw . . .

BARBS *gives her a mock clip round the ear.*

BARBS. *And* I want you to chuck out that keechy wash away the
grey home colorant from your bathroom cabinet! I could take
years off you. Come into the salon, how many times do I have
to tell you, we'll colour it, nothing roary, it'll be a really subtle
mesh of lowlights and highlights –

ALICE. Och, I don't know that I'd suit dyed hair. Don't get me
wrong, *you* do, but –

BARBS. Come on try this, this'll suit you, it's a wee Sara
Sturgeon out of Moon –

ALICE. Barbs, my own frock will do me fine –

BARBS. Put it on. Let me see it on you. Or will I get yon
Armani . . . ?

ALICE. No!

BARBS. You could huv that, it's only Emporio.

Surveys what ALICE *has got into.*

BARBS. Mmm. Maybe . . . That's nice and simple, but it hings
well. Keep it, I never wear it anyway, I bought it during my

shopaholic phase when I'd put weight on, it's no me.That's better. That's much better. Perfect. You look great!

ALICE. Barbs, don't mammy me! (*Beat.*) I'm fine the way I am.

BARBS. Christ, I am as bad as my own fucking mother!

ALICE. Barbs listen . . .

BARBS. Lonely. That's why I want a baby, Alice. I feel empty. I feel lonely.

ALICE. Well, children don't stop you from feeling lonely.

BARBS. Well, what does then?

ALICE. Work.

BARBS. And what exactly does my work contribute to the sum of human happiness? Sweet fuck all . . .

ALICE. Quite a lot I should think.

A rueful laugh –

BARBS. At least if I make an arse of it I could make somebody miserable . . . For months.

ALICE *is looking in the mirror. She whirls in delight.*

ALICE. Honestly, Barbs darlin', it's amazing! Total transformation! You've got me so I would hardly know myself so I wouldny! Can I borrow it? Please? I won't keep it, no, but can I get a loan of it? For the night? Please?

BARBS *shakes her head, speechless. Of course she can.*

ALICE. Barbs. Listen . . . It wasn't my toyboy. He was my son . . .

Black.

Music bridge: 'Don't Make Me Over' by Dionne Warwick ('Accept me for what I am. Accept me for the things that I do'.)

Scene Two

Semi dark of all day emptiness. On the middle of the table is a single 'To a Daughter' birthday card.

Door opens, BARBS enters, slams door, sighs theatrically, walks over to coffee table, puts a pile of cards and other mail down without opening yet, picks up the birthday card, opens it and shuts it to activate the cassio-tone tinny little version of the anthem she sings along to, quite enjoying acting out the self pity.

BARBS. Happy birthday to me
  Happy birthday to me
  Happy birthday dear Barbs-ie
  Happy birthday to me.

  She rotates her stiff neck, picks up the blue vodka bottle from the table and has a quick neat swig.

  A big leather armchair swivels round. in it, an open copy of Hello magazine in front of her, is BARBS's mother, SADIE.

SADIE. How much are you paying for fabric softener these days?

BARBS. Jesus, Mum –

SADIE. There was a two giant size for the price of one offer in the supermarket last week, so I brought you one over, pet.

BARBS. – I nearly shat a brick.

SADIE. Language.

BARBS. Mum I have told you I don't want you coming here cleaning. I've got a cleaner.

SADIE. A lick and a spit. Does nothing!

BARBS. Sitting there in the bloody dark scaring me half –

SADIE. I just sat down for five minutes with the Hello while I was waiting for the kitchen floor to dry so's I could jiffywax it and here I must've went and fell –

BARBS. – I don't want my own mother working as a cleaner.

SADIE. It wasny that when it was a matter of your ballet -tap-and-highland.

BARBS. I was eight. Jesus.

  It's a Tuesday.

SADIE. Your birthday.

BARBS. You always come on a Thursday.

SADIE. That's correct, the state that so-called Thingwy leaves your work surfaces in on a Wednesday just as well I pop up on a Thursday, pet. Damp disgrace. I'd do it twice as well for half the price.

BARBS. No way!

SADIE. Is that all the thanks I get? Traipsing all the way over here, waiting ver near an hour for a forty-eight, just to gie your penthouse a wee birthday hoover . . .

BARBS. Mum, I'm very grateful –

SADIE. Exactly. By the way hen, here's a wee present. Happy birthday, Barbara.

BARBS *takes the present and looks at it. Apprehensive.*

SADIE. Course you'll likely no like it.

BARBS *opens the present with composed pleasure. She Finds a horrific hot pink acrylic garment with appliqued pearls. She looks at it. A beat then simultaneously.*

SADIE/BARBS. You don't like it! / It's lovely!

SADIE. You don't.

BARBS. I do! Gorgeous!

SADIE. Try it on.

BARBS. After . . . I'm sure it'll fit me . . .

SADIE. Come on, let me see it on you.

SADIE *won't give in till* BARBS *does.* BARBS *tries to resist her, then begins to get out of her own top and into* SADIE'*s present . . .*

SADIE. I says to Mina next door, I says, she'll likely no like it, I says, I don't know what she *does* like. It'll likely no be dreich enough to please her. Gorgeous shade isn't it? Unusual. I've the exact same one in turquoise.

It's mohair and acrylic. I bought the wool and Mina knitted it for you. Washes like a ribbon. That's what Mina says. And she's from Hawick, knows her jumpers.

BARBS. Inside out.

SADIE. Eh?

BARBS. Nothing.

SADIE. She does, but. Presser in Pringles. Says she wouldn't give cashmere house room. This is softer. Brushed.

BARBS *struggles into the awful jumper.* SADIE *produces some magazines, an incongruous mix of 'Peoples' Friend' and 'Hello!'.*

SADIE. That's better. That's much better. That's a bit cheerier for your birthday. I brought you over a few Hellos and Mina sent over some old Friends she was finished with.

BARBS. Eh?

SADIE. Have you got them?

BARBS. No.

SADIE. No I didny think so.

BARBS. Mum –

SADIE *holds up the Hello magazine from her lap.*

SADIE. I was just reading there that thon Princess Marie Kristen of Sweden's developed an eating disorder.

BARBS. – Mum, it's my birthday, lets pop out for a wee bite and a glass of bubbly.

SADIE. Course, the Friend is right aulfashioned but Mina likes it. I don't think emdy in the People's Friend's ever heard of bulimia . . . But, och, if you don't want them yourself you can always take them into the salon, save you a few bob's worth of glossies.

BARBS. Anyway, c'mon . . .

BARBS*'s hands go to the waistband as she prepares to strip off her horrific jumper.* SADIE *sees this.* BARBS *sees her seeing.* BARBS*'s hands leave the waistband immediately, she smooths jumper down.*

BARBS. C'mon, I'll wear my new jumper, you stick on a wee lick of lipstick and we'll pop over the road to the Italian Centre, nothing fancy, they do a lovely focaccia and roasted vegetables.

SADIE. Ach, where is the enjoyment for me in that?

BARBS *gives in deflated.*

SADIE. So, can I get a fag? Seeing as it's your birthday . . .

BARBS *goes and fetches and ironically presents an ashtray.*

SADIE. You never said thankyou for your card.

BARBS. Thankyou.

She flaps it open and shut to air the cassio-tone Happy Birthday again and puts it back down on the coffee table.

SADIE. Zat all you got?

BARBS. No, there's all these.

SADIE. You've never opened them.

BARBS. I haven't had the bloody chance.

SADIE. Did Davie send you one?

BARBS. Did Davie ever send me one? In twenty years did he ever send me one? Davie phoned.

SADIE. When?

BARBS. This morning.

SADIE. What did he say?

BARBS. He said happy bloody birthday, what did you think he'd say?

SADIE. Did he?

BARBS. He did. Actually he said he was sorry he forgot to send me a card this year, doll, I said he was sorry he never sent me a card every year, he said to listen to the Mystic Memories slot on Radio Clyde because he had put in a request for me when he was up at the D.J.'s flat selling him a Lalique lamp for his burd's birthday, I said Radio Clyde gave me the boke, I was a James Naughtie and John Thingwy fan in the morning, he said suit yoursel but gie it a wee go, but! Because he had a feeling the D.J. might play it, see, and he couldnae listen to it hissel because he was on the motorway in England somewhere driving up a load of gash shoes from a fire damaged factory in Northampton for his pal Peem then he must've drove under a motorway bridge or something because the signal on his mobile began to break up and that was about it although if I mind of anything else I'll put it down in writing for you, Mum, OK?

SADIE. You broke that boy's heart . . .

BARBS. I broke *his* – mother, let's have a drink, it's my birthday, there's a bottle in the fridge.

BARBS *exits to kitchen, is back in no time ready to pop it.*

BARBS. Here, look, Mummmm's, it's got your name on it.

SADIE. By the way, I was tidying up your bathroom cabinet and that old tube of spermicidal cream next to your Dutch cap was past its sell-by date. I chucked it out for you.

BARBS. Thanks . . .

BARBS *pops the champagne. Her mother sips, wrinkles up her nose.* BARBS *ignores this through gritted teeth.*

BARBS. Mmmm.

She shuts her eyes and lies back.

SADIE. Anyway, pet, did you have a nice day?

BARBS. Mmm, I had a lovely day.

I had a super day, and gosh it's getting better and better as it goes on, well, there was a surprise Buck's fizz *brunch* for me, and here had all my employees not clubbed together for the biggest bouquet you ever saw in all your puff, Stefan was utterly charming all day, *didn't* do any skiving, *never* mentioned the products problem, never nipped my head over the stupit franchising idea, never let a patronising syllable pass his lips, never managed to get up my nose at all. I had a perfect day.

SADIE. No much point sending you a card you don't even bother to open them. I suppose I should be flattered you opened mines . . .

BARBS. Mum, you sent yours three days early with do not open till the 29th all over it, these just arrived today, presumably after I left for work, because I do have to work, you know, being the boss means you are in earlier, not later, OK? but I will certainly open them right now, and see who if anybody, still loves me. Four people, eh, och, well that's better than nothing –

BARBS *opens one.*

BARBS. Howard. Howard next door.

SADIE. He's good appearance –

BARBS. He's moved out! Fancy Howard remembering.
Correction, Howard no doubt has a computer programme
which remembers for him. Oh and this one is from Jane Izzard
and all the Production team at Morningtime Makeover, that's
very personal, wonder why I don't have one from the Bank, or
the Taj Mahal Deliver-A-Curry, they always send me a lovely
Christmas Card . . . Oh, *Alice,* lots of love from Alice, Tommy,
and family. That's nice.

SADIE. Alice? Alice Marshall?

BARBS. Alice Inglis, Alice Marshall as was, uh huh.

SADIE. Davie's sister Alice?

BARBS. The same.

SADIE. You still see Alice?

BARBS. Ma, you know I do! We go to the aerobics. I told you
I cut her hair a couple of weeks ago.

SADIE. How is she?

BARBS. Alice? Oh . . . Alice is fine. Fantastic, as a matter of fact.
Blossoming . . . Anyway, Alice Pal, you remembered . . .

BARBS *drinks then opens fourth card.*

BARBS. Oh, but Noelene's sent me one anyway! No need for the
And Family Alice, Noelene's done it herself. One from her and
Andrea.

SADIE *takes the card. She doesn't get it.*

SADIE. *'Oh no I forgot to have children'* . . . ?

BARBS. It's out the feminist bookshop.

SADIE. I don't get it.

BARBS. It's supposed to be a joke. Noelene's only seventeen.

SADIE. Aw . . .

She puts the card out on the table. A beat or two of silence.

SADIE. I met the girl Macalinden there.

BARBS. Uh-huh . . .

SADIE. You mind the lassie Macalinden?

BARBS. No.

SADIE. You do.

BARBS. I don't.

SADIE. Passed on her youngest daughter's Brownie tunic to you,
I was up all night unpicking the Pixies badge and sewing on
the Scottish Kelpies the night before the Armistice Parade.

BARBS. Mum I don't remember . . .

SADIE. Aye you do. Brown Owl said no harm to the woman, but
her Melting Moments weren't a patch on mines.

BARBS. Eh . . . ?

SADIE. This is gey wersh isn't it? The only champagne I like the
taste of's Babycham.

BARBS. You mean this 'Girl Macalinden' is about sixty.

SADIE. Oh she'll be more than that! Year ahead of me at the
school. Anyway she was asking for you.

BARBS. That's nice.

SADIE. Said she'd seen you on Morningtime Makeover and she'd
thought you did wonders for that woman that was just out the
jail.

BARBS. Good.

SADIE. Uh-huh, she said to me your Barbra's never off the TV.

BARBS. I wouldn't say that . . .

SADIE. She says to me: plus I see 'Barbs Marshall' was the
Celebrity Starscope in the Sunday Mail last week, I says yes,
she says big changes ahead if there's anything in it, I says our
Barbra is not superstitious.

BARBS. I bloody am.

SADIE. She says to me had you a man? I said not as such. Och
and anyway what would you be wanting with a man with your
lifestyle. I says Barbara's got a career, I says she co-owns a
salon, she's never off the telly, she's got a life of her own and
four weeks in a Luxury Timeshare on the nice bit of the
Algarve. I says our Barbra's perfectly happy.

BARBS. I'm not.

SADIE. Aye you are!

BARBS. Jesus Christ on a bike.

SADIE. She was saying to me did I not want grandchildren? I said
what did I want grandchildren for? I've got grandchildren! Our
Megan, Darren and Patrice.

BARBS. In New South Wales . . .

SADIE. Well, I've seen them. Except wee Patrice.

BARBS. Mum, I'll go into the travel agent's tomorrow and get
you a ticket to Australia if that's what you want.

SADIE. Ocht no pet. It's all barbecues. I'm not a big barbecue
hand. Not at my age.

BARBS. Mum, honestly, how old are you?

SADIE. Sixty-one.

BARBS. That's not old.

SADIE. Oh is it not? Wish I'd had your chances. Career. Travel.
Own home. Wish I'd done something with my life instead of
just frittering it away bringing up you and Our Billy.

BARBS. Mum.

SADIE. I was a widow before I was thirty.

BARBS. Christ, mother I wish you wouldn't always say that:
'I was a widow before I was thirty'.

SADIE. I was. I was a widow before my thirtieth birthday.

BARBS. OK. But . . . Bloody saying it like that. 'My Life
Story' . . .

SADIE. It's not a story, it's a fact. You and Billy were my whole
life.

BARBS. I know, I know . . .

SADIE. Not old? Sometimes I feel bloody ancient I'll tell you.

BARBS. Well I bet you do. Cause so do I. The day for instance.
Bloody ancient. But I'm not actually. I'm thirty-nine. I wish it
wasn't my bloody birthday, because I can't stand thinking
about the next one. I don't see how I can possibly be pushing
forty when I still don't even know what I want to be when
I grow up.

SADIE. Peak of your profession! Fabulous salary!

BARBS. I don't have a salary. You don't even know what a salary is do you? I have a business. I have *half* a business. That could go down the tubes, like any other business. Stefan might bulldozer me into this stupit franchise idea of his. Over my dead body, but you never know. Plus fashion is fickle, face it. The now we're the flavour of the month, next year for all we know the last place anybody will come to get their hair done is Razor City. I've seen it before. That daft horoscope could be right. Everything might change. I might meet a fabulous rich old man. I might meet a fabulous younger man. I might go and work among the slums of South America, drive a lorryful of food to Bosnia, I might buy myself silicone tits, I might do the Open University. Ach I might arse around exactly the same neither here nor there from one wee minicrisis to the next. Or I might do *something*.

I might decide to have a baby on my own –

SADIE. – Don't be stupid –

BARBS. – I might do *something*. I might be happy. I might be bloody miserable. But I'll tell you one thing. I refuse to pretend to be happy so you can be happy about how happy I am, OK?

SADIE. I don't think you like that jumper I bought you. If you don't like it, just give it back to me and I'll wear it for working in, pet.

BARBS. Mum, I love the jumper.

SADIE. You don't, I can tell.

BARBS. I do. I do.

SADIE. Nor have you said if you enjoyed your strippogram.

BARBS. So it was you!

SADIE. Ach, you ought to lighten up. Be a wee bit broadminded. I am. Mina and I might go the Guild Outing to the Chippendales.

Black.

Music bridge: Clare Grogan's 'Happy Birthday to You, Happy Birthday.'

Scene Three

*Later the same night. Tinfoil catering packages and mess across
the coffee table among the birthday cards.* BRENDAN BOYLE,
BARBS'*s best friend* (*gorgeous – but gay of course*) *and* BARBS
*have just demolished a Chinese meal and their first bottle of
champagne. He is in mid mock harangue of* BARBS, *who he's
really got squirming.*

BRENDAN. . . . *So* she's only the wee shampoo lassie and
sweeper upper, right? Sixteen and seldom been shagged –

BARBS. Don't!

BRENDAN. – Nice enough wee lassie –

BARBS. I know . . .

BRENDAN. – Nice wee lassie wee Kimberly! Poor wee
Kimberly, the Sowell, Whit does she know? Nothing.

So she's well into it. Giving it that. And we haven't the heart,
huv we, to go Heard It Heard It? We're like dead polite. We're
like all agog. As if. She's like: 'the shampoo girl's just rinsed
off the conditioner at the backwash when she sees the guys
hauns gaun like that, right? Under his robe. Hits him a clatter
roon the back of the heid with the shampoo spray, lays him oot
cold, and here it turns oot – '

You swan in and go: 'He was only polishing his glasses!'

BARBS. Och stop it.

BRENDAN. You go: 'Kimberly. Kindly, before you come out with
all this keech from your day-release classes, before you bore
your colleagues with jejeune reruns of ancient urban myths
concerning Panda cars, cats with internal injuries keeling over
and snuffing it after eating innocent dinner party leftovers, or
women dying of heart attacks when they see the dog devouring
the turkey giblets their son has stuffed down their drunken
husband's flies – *kindly* check with us, Kimberly, you goes,
whether we've heard this one before, eh? You will probably
find the answer is: Many Times. Many, many times. Right?'

You go: 'I – for one – have got an eight-thirty. Has nobody *else*
around here got work to go to?' And off you go. El Boss
Barbara 'Claus' Barbie wi your face like fizz.

We're like that.

Wee Kimberly's like . . . ooyah! Pure scarlet.

I'm like: I wonder who shat in her handbag?

BARBS. I am a monster . . .

BRENDAN. I mean, Barbs, give us a break, if you don't even give us a clue how are we supposed to mind it's your birthday? We would've done something, obviously –

BARBS. A complete monster.

BRENDAN. Sure are Barbo. But then so were all the women I adore. Bette Davis. Joan Crawford . . .

BRENDAN *and* BARBS. . . . Marilyn Monroe. Princess Diana. Judy Garland . . .

BARBS. And you, Brendan, you are totally a complete Nelly cliché.

BRENDAN. Totally. But then you see, growing up a Glesga Boy in No Mean City – yeah, among all the easy-affrontit Mammies and all the Daddies that were pure frozen arsed hardmen wi jaws made oot o girders, well, I found out very early that the world and its wife were quite happy and totally tane oan wi the local token Wee-Bit-of-a-Mary-Anne-God-Love-Him. Even Father Hugh And Father Thomas used to pure crease themsels at my antics when I took centre stage crossdressed at the Legion of Mary Conversazzione.

Anyway some of us might be clichés, but we are seldom short of a shag.

BARBS. Ooyah. Unike certain other folk, you mean? OK, Brendan, you bastard, ye, don't rub it in.

Sometimes I doubt I'll ever have sex again.

BRENDAN. Eh?

BARBS. I mean it. I mean there is bound to be a last time isn't there? I mean, there is bound to be a last time, in your life, but you would tend to hope that, unlike the first time, you wouldny know it while it was happening because you'd think Christ this better be good.

BRENDAN. You're mad.

BARBS. How?

BRENDAN. Look at you. Sexy as fuck.

BARBS. Yeah . . . Says you. What would *you* know?

BRENDAN. I know. Drop dead fucking gorgeous.

BARBS. Old.

BRENDAN. Bollox.

BARBS. I am. Ancient. Thirty-nine. This is my fortieth year, Brendan . . .

BRENDAN. You don't look it, but.

BARBS. I feel it. After a day like the day and a night like the night. My mother. My mother would put years on you . . .

Anyway it was very very kind of you to make an Auld Wummin very happy and schlepp up here wi that bottle of champagne and carry-out chinky. Who cares if I never see another willie as long as there is Sechaun King Prawns?

She skewers a last one out of the tinfoil with her chopstick and devours.

BRENDAN. Ooyah!

BARBS. Crunch. Crunch.

BRENDAN. No wonder men forget you. Correction no wonder men have bad dreams about you, no wonder they hit the grunn running and don't stop till they've got the protection of ten doted wee blonde dollybirds between them and big bad brainy women with sharp tongues and sharp teeth like you.

BARBS. Oh, speaking of doted wee blonde dollybirds, that wee model Stefan is shacking up with is up the duff apparently.

BRENDAN. Christ, is there nae end to that prick's fecundity?

BARBS. Apparently not. Over the moon according to Tiff.

BRENDAN. Has he forgot he's got five already plus an ex wife that's drinking herself to death in Drymen?

BARBS. That was Tash's point exactly but Tiff says dee-lighted. Like a cat with two tails.

BRENDAN. Dog!

BARBS. Now I wouldn't say that she is a gorgeous looking lassie!

They both laugh.

BRENDAN. You should ditch Stefan and open up a new wan wi me. He doesny know where it's at these days. The cutting edge, that's moi.

BARBS. Last prawn?

BRENDAN. – You should but!

No takers in either direction. She skewers the prawn, devours.

BARBS. They were quite delicious. Thank you.

(At some unspecified time during this scene BRENDAN must clear away to the kitchen the debris of this meal. If she's not too distracted at that time she might even help him.)

BRENDAN. You're very welcome. Many happy returns.

He raises his glass to her.

BARBS. But was it entirely kindly meant, I wonder, to bring us a bottle of Youth Dew and a copy of Germaine Greer's book on the menopause?

BRENDAN. Gie's a brekk, time I'd finished that full head high-lights and you'd finally let us oot of work the night, ya bliddy slavedriver ye, there was bugger all open except Waterstone's and the Nine O Clock Chemists on the corner, and it was either that or a box of foosty Quality Street oot the Asian Grocer's for which I did not think you'd thank me.

BARBS. But I do thank you, Brendan. You're a darling.

BRENDAN. I was gonny get you that 'Men Are From Mars Women Are From Venus' but I thought to myself –

BARBS/BRENDAN. – Read it!

They nod simultaneously.

BARBS. I've also read that 'Women Who Love Too Much', 'The Cinderella Syndrome', 'The Rules', 'The Little Book of Calm', 'Promises Lovers Make When It's Getting Late', 'Why Women Need Chocolate' and 'Feel the Fear And Do It Anyway'.

I was going to write one of my own: 'Women Who Fancy Men So That Is Them Fucked Forget It' . . . Yup. I've read them all, *plus* 'Rosemary Connelly's Hip And Thigh Diet', but this is still me, since yesterday . . .

BRENDAN. Fuck you got on anyway?

BARBS. Don't start me.

BRENDAN. Great taste your mother!

BARBS. Fabulous. But listen, it really was nice of you . . .

BRENDAN. Ach . . .

BARBS. No honestly . . .

BRENDAN. I was dead dead sorry I'd forgot. You never forget mines.

BARBS. I thought I wanted it just to go by me, unmarked and unremarked on, then when that big bouquet arrived at work – and it would be today – for flaming Tash . . .

BRENDAN. Tiff –

BARBS. Tiff or Tash, whoever . . . Anyway, I was disappointed I have to admit it, but, see, when yon bloody birthday strippogram arrived, Christ I could've seen *him* far enough.

BRENDAN. I thought he was quite cute.

BARBS. I know you did. Capone-ogram! Capone O Gram. My bloody mother. That Full Monty's got a lot to answer for I'll tell you . . . 'Parently he's a boy Binnie, brought up a Plymouth Brethren but got elbowed out the fold when he set up as a strippogram. Originally under the Enterprise allowance scheme according to my bloody mother. Who got suckered into clubbing together with Mina next door on his This Month Special Offer Two for The Price of One. Uh-huh. Mina sent her Auld Mammy a Birthday Tarzanogram up at the Eastern Star Whist Drive. Brought the house down. Poor guy was lucky to get out alive.

BRENDAN. Well, he does have a tasty torso. As we all saw. I was like ooyah! Get that waashed and brung round to my winnebago.

BARBS. Don't! I was in the middle of Carol Smillie's lo-lights, I could have Saint Valentine's Day *Massacred* the bugger . . . Talk about a right rid neck . . .

BRENDAN. Ach lighten up.

BARBS. Don't you start.

BARBS. Plus – what a day – there would have to be yon Mother
Of The Bride that I was in the same class as in Primary School.
As she would keep flaming reminding me.

BRENDAN. You're joking! She was ancient.

BARBS. Same age as me.

BRENDAN. Nah! Her that got the Bergen Beige Blonde foils and
the graduated bob? That Big Fat Wan? Wi the face like a burst
tomatta? Her that was the spitting image of Rab C. Nesbitt? I
had to bite my tongue no to say to her: See you and Rab C?
Youse could be *sisters*.

BARBS. Well her and me could be twins. 'Cept I'm six month
older than her.

BRENDAN. Get tae!

BARBS. Brendan do I look as old as her?

BRENDAN. I'm no even gonny answer that.

A beat or two.

BARBS. I lied to my mother.

BRENDAN. Oh-wah! What about, Barbsie?

BARBS. I do. I do know what I want to do next. I want to have a
baby.

BRENDAN. You asking?

BARBS. You dancing?

BRENDAN *has caught up. Is silenced. Looks away.* BARBS
wanders, picks up her wedding photograph. Puts it down.

BARBS. What's the matter with me. I should be divorced. This
should be put away in a drawer.

BRENDAN *comes over, takes it off her, looks at it, looks at her,
puts it back down on the table.*

BRENDAN. Nice. It's a nice photy, Barbs. Of both y you . . .
Apart fae the His'n'Her matching feather haircuts. Fuck-
sake . . .

But BARBS *is unreachable. To herself –*

BARBS. When I was nineteen I married Davie. Nineteen. Christ, I couldnae even walk right in high heels . . .

BRENDAN. I like Davie.

BARBS. I like Davie. Liking him isny the problem. I married him to get away from my mammy. Plus I fancied myself entering my twenties as a grown up married lady . . .

When I was twenty-nine I left Davie. Well I fancied myself entering my thirties as a swinging single career woman unencumbered by an ageing hippy that couldn't seem to grasp that this was the nineteen freaking eighties.

And now I'm thirty nine . . .

BRENDAN *looks away from her. Nodding.*

BARBS. I do. I want to have a baby.

Silence. They are not looking at each other. BRENDAN *nods again.*

BARBS. I mean my biological clock –

BRENDAN. I ken, Germaine . . .

BARBS. I never used to. Do you remember that advert in the pictures? For hot dogs? 'An hour from now you'll wish you'd had one.' I used to think, that'll be me, one day I'll wake up old and grey and childless and I'll wish I'd had one, but –

BRENDAN. You . . . wereny hungry?

BARBS. Nope. But see now? All of a sudden . . . I'm ravenous!

I want a baby. But who with, that is the question?

BRENDAN. How about that guy from the Citizen's Theatre?

BARBS. Brendan, he was more interested in cheap haircuts than sex.

BRENDAN. Well, there's Handsome we met in the lift yon time. He was all over you.

BARBS. Howard? He's flitted –

BRENDAN. – That's a sin, 'cause –

BARBS. – And, please. I really would have to have been helluva desperate to have shagged Howard.

BRENDAN. I'd shag him.

BARBS. You'd shag anything.

BRENDAN. Please. That is very hurtful. I'm gonna turn over a new leaf and find myself a deep and meaningful.

BARBS. Hah.

BRENDAN. You wait and see. Anyway you were talking about a sperminator. Shouldn't be difficult. What's the problem? You could just ask somebody –

BARBS. Brendan, I *am* asking.

BRENDAN. Oh.

BARBS. Listen, Brendan, do not assume – necessarily – that I want – necessarily – to have the baby the old fashioned way where the father is present at the conception.

BRENDAN. Oh, you mod-ren girls . . . !

BARBS. I mean all I absolutely need is a well timed syringeful of spunk that I can keep warm in a jar up my jumper until I get the chance to skoosh it up. (*Beat.*) Cool!

BRENDAN. What?

BARBS. I don't want to keep it *warm* up my jumper, sorry, I want to keep it cool, don't I? Cold. In my knickers presumably. (*Beat.*) Brendan, it is basically just like being a blood donor.

BRENDAN. Barbs, it is not 'just like being a blood donor'.

BARBS. I'd buy you the magazine!

BRENDAN. Hah!

BARBS. Just . . . don't reject it out of hand.

BRENDAN. 'Overheard at a party!' (*Beat.*) Sorry.

BARBS. No, Brendan, I'm sorry . . .

BRENDAN. No, don't be sorry . . . I'll . . . think about it. I will think about it, but I don't think I'll think about it very seriously. (*Beat.*) Sorry . . .

BARBS. That is quite OK.

BRENDAN. Sure?

BARBS. Yup.

Anyway, dear heart, excuse me, but I have to go to bed now. because I am bushed. Pished and bushed.

BRENDAN. Oh, that's OK. Because I've got a date.

BARBS. So late? A Date? *Who* with?

BRENDAN. Oh God. You'll never guess!

BARBS. Fuck, I don't know. Richard Gere. My Davie. *Tell* me.

BRENDAN. Guess!

BARBS. I can't. (*Beat.*) Oh yes I can. I'm getting pinstripe suit . . . I'm getting fedora . . . black and white two tone correspondent shoes . . . I'm getting a bulging posing pouch . . . (*Laughing.*) My fucking mother's strippogram. For me! For me you bugger! Bren-dan, Brendan, Brendan! . . . What's his name?

BRENDAN. Cammy . . .

BARBS. As in – *Knicker?*

BRENDAN. Naw as in *Cameron.* Cameron Binnie. A *Prodd*estant I hud presumed, but you know me, I'm no fussy, I've tried all creeds and colours, the hale gammy . . .

BARBS. How did this come about?

BRENDAN. Well, you know how you hunted him?

BARBS. I sure did. Carol fucking Smillie laughing up her sleeve at me!

BRENDAN. Well he came back. While you were out for lunch. Looking for his Kipper tie. Plus in the caffuffle he'd lost wan of the knobs aff his tommy gun. We got chatt'n. This and that. Blah blah. And blabbity . . . So, eh, it's an ill wind.

BARBS. Aye, that blaws nae cunt fuck all good.

She is laughing and shooing him out the door.

BARBS. En-joy.

BRENDAN. Sleep tight.

BRENDAN *turns to go. Whirls back in to close to* BARBS.

BRENDAN. Well, what do I know, it isny my biological clock, but, haw, Barbs, are you not panicking far too early? I mean, my Auntie Sybill had a wean at fifty-four, didny even know she was expecting, thought it was a bad plate of wulks on the Maid Of The Loch, but it wisny.

BARBS. And was the baby all right?

BRENDAN. Christ no! Fact he was a congenital every syndrome in the Medical Dictionary, wee Freddie . . .

BRENDAN *perks up.*

BRENDAN. But he might not have been!

BARBS *is laughing.*

Fade to black.

Music bridge: Doctor Hook's 'Who's Gonna Iron My Shirts? Who's Gonna Kiss Me Where It Hurts? (If Not You).'

Scene Four

In BARBS*'s empty place it is intimately lit, an ice bucket has appeared on the table with a bottle of champagne sticking out of it. The telephone rings, answer machine kicks in.*

BARBS, *a Japanese kimono falling open over her seduction undies, sticks her head round the door to listen to who it is, then immediately she re-exits towards the bathroom without picking up when it's only her mother.*

SADIE*'s voice speaks out. Awkward, uncomfortable. Too loud.*

SADIE'S VOICE. Hello. Hello, this is Mrs. Sadie Kirkwood leaving a message for Barbara Marshall . . .

Hello? Hello? Hello are you there? I hate this thing . . .
Eh, Barbara? Emm I was wondering . . . Mina's wee Club is looking for speakers. They've a good speaker for next week, it's the Home Economics teacher up the high school doing food hygiene in the light of E-Coli, and the week after they thought they'd got old Mr. Simpson that used to run the Co doing his slides of his safari up the Zambesi, but, here, he's been taken in for tests, so I volunteered you in as an emergency. Nothing complicated. Mibbe a makeover or a make up demonstration. Anything. Celebrity gossip . . . The sort of thing

you can do standing on your head, Barbara. Let me know if you canny manage it, OK?

During this last BARBS *has re-entered still in her kimono with her whole face covered in a white or pale greenish facemask and has been advancing towards the machine, glaring murderously at it.*

A daft pause then an abrupt and weirdly formal –

SADIE'S VOICE. Thank you!

It clicks off –

BARBS. Nae tother a baw! Christ, mother, if you don't take the fucking shortbread biscuit . . .

BARBS *goes out to the kitchen brings cutlery for two, napkins, lights candles, quite unconsciously singing away to herself (no conscious agenda, it's only the CD she's just been playing, that's all) the old Scott Walker classic, 'Make It Easy on Yourself . . . ' without ever quite completing the 'Cause breakin' up is so hard to do' line. The ground floor buzzer rings.*

BARBS. Christ . . .

BARBS *looks at her watch in horror. Goes and presses intercom.*

BARBS. Hello?

VOICE OVER INTERCOM. It's me . . .

BARBS. Jesus, Davie you're early.

The inside doorbell shrills, and, fastening the sash of the kimono round her and climbing on to some high silly mules, she opens the door to DAVIE MARSHALL, *41, in a smart and stylish suit and holding a couple of old plastic carrier bags.*

BARBS. Yonks early by the way!

DAVIE. That's nice, doll! No that much, we says seven, right.

BARBS. Half seven. It's ten to! Plus you're always *late*. I can depend on it . . .

DAVIE. Well, I've turned over a new leaf, doll, how are you? You're looking *pale* . . .

He finds this funny. BARBS *looks in the mirror, remembers her facemask. But is buggered if she's going to take it off early because he's here. It's only* DAVIE.

BARBS. Anyway, a drink. Now you're here. How are *you?* Davie, I wouldn't have recognised you. You look great.

BARBS *moves towards the wine in the ice bucket.*

DAVIE. Open this!

He hands her a parcel, hastily and shambolically wrapped in newspaper and a third hand polythene poke.

She pulls out a junkshop treasure of a framed blow up of the classic kids' shoe ad of the fifties. Back view, a wee boy and girl walk off into the sunset . . .

BARBS. The Startrite kids!

DAVIE. Don't smile, then. Your face'll crack!

BARBS. Thank you, Davie, you're a darling so you are . . . What's it in aid of?

DAVIE. Nothing. I just thought it was you. Go wi thon Bisto Kids thing – have you still got that up in the kitchen?

BARBS. Nuh.

DAVIE. Naw? Oh . . . Plus I brung you up some classic vinyl.

She removes an LP in a beat up cover.

BARBS. The Lovin' Spoonful . . . ?

DAVIE. You loved thame.

BARBS. Oh so I did . . .

DAVIE. Aye. You were into sixties retro by the seventies. Before your time so you were! Put it on.

BARBS. After.

DAVIE. Well, long time no see, eh? When did I last see you? Been ages, doll. I've phoned you several times. You're never ever in . . .

BARBS. I wouldn't say that.

DAVIE. I've left you messages several times, but did you phone me back . . . ? Nuh . . .

BARBS. Anyway, when did you get the haircut?

DAVIE. Ach, it was time. I thought to myself I don't want to look like wan of they sad bastards. The auld baldy wans wi the scraggy wee ponytails . . .

BARBS. You look great, you really do. *Plus* the suit . . .

She picks out the bottle of champagne from the icebucket, but just as she goes to untwist the wire –

DAVIE. Eh, doll, don't open that for me. You any mineral water or anything? Appletise? I mean obviously if you want it –

BARBS. You not drinking?

DAVIE. I'm not, no . . .

BARBS. Wow. Anything you should tell me?

DAVIE. No really. Nuh.

She shrugs and puts the bottle unopened back into the bucket. As she exits kitchenward –

BARBS. Mineral water it is. It'll do me good a night on the wagon an all.

DAVIE. Anyway, my big sister was telling me she was round, you done her hair for her?

BARBS *reappears with an almost empty plastic bottle of Highland Spring and pours it into the two wine glasses.*

BARBS. You've seen her?

DAVIE. I have yes . . .

BARBS. This is flat . . . Ach, It's likely too flat, Davie, I'm sorry . . .

DAVIE. How did you think she was?

BARBS. Did she, eh, tell you? –

DAVIE. Aye, she did, yeah . . . What did you think?

BARBS*'s face says she was gobsmacked. She shakes her head.*

BARBS. I mean, how could she have kept that a secret for all these years . . . ? I mean it was a secret? You never ever mentioned anything about it . . .

DAVIE. I knew nothing. Nothing at all. Although looking back . . . I was only, what? Fourteen year aul' at the time but I mind Alice was 'working away from home', that was the story.

See when you saw her? What did you think?

BARBS. What did you think yourself . . . ?

DAVIE. I think that cunt's at it!

BARBS. The boy? But she was really –

DAVIE. Some boy. He's a grown man. Just swanning back into her life after – whit – twenty-five year because he's 'curious about his roots'? Never mind what kind of a havoc – do you know she's *told* Tommy by the way, and introduced him to him. *And* the girls . . .

BARBS. Surely Tommy knew?

DAVIE. Oh, course he *knew*. Haw, how do you think Noelene and Andrea felt all of a sudden having this half brother they'd never even heard of?

BARBS. Did you ask them?

DAVIE. No.

BARBS. Did you ask Alice?

DAVIE. She said they were delighted.

BARBS. Well then . . .

DAVIE. Did she tell you whose wean it was?

BARBS. She did, yes . . .

Very forcefully –

DAVIE. The worst badyin in the whole scheme, Hannegan. Why on earth would she –

BARBS. But, Davie, he was very handsome. Very clever and all. It takes brains to be a villain, and he was very charming with it. Could be . . . when he wanted to . . .

DAVIE. Well, he came to a very sticky end anyway.

BARBS. I wonder how Alice's boy felt to hear all that?

DAVIE. Well, I hope he was satisfied.

BARBS. Have you met him yet?

DAVIE. No. No and I don't want to.

BARBS. Davie, Alice is absolutely over the moon!

He remains unconvinced.

DAVIE. Anyway, I wanted to tell you my big news. When last was I in touch with you? –

BARBS. My birthday.

DAVIE. So it was, so it was, doll. Hey, did you like your record?

BARBS. What? That request? God that DJ! Yuch. All that slush about 'it was twenty years ago today that Barbara and Davie walked down the aisle, she was only a teenager at the time and that boy wasn't a whole lot older, but that boy and that girl they couldn't have loved each other more' . . .

DAVIE. I thought you'd like it. It was anonymous, the Mystic Memories slot – only you and me knew what it was about, Barbra . . .

BARBS. Christ.

DAVIE. I thought you'd be pleased.

BARBS. 'There's been a lot of water under the bridge, *he's* had other relationships' – yeah, not fucking half, starting from a year after the wedding when you were never off the road with those ginks in that band –

DAVIE. We nearly made it. (*Pause.*) We came that close to getting the record deal.

BARBS. – '*She's* had other relationships.' – Yeah, but not till after we split up!

DAVIE. That's what split us up. That 'affair' you had. Coming to me and telling me you were 'having an affair' . . . I never had an affair. The girls in the van after the gigs were not an affair . . .

BARBS. 'But he wanted me to tell Barbara: Happy Birthday and to remember that in all his life there'll only ever be one you.'

I was choked, Davie. It got to me, I must admit. Tell you, I was stood there in my kitchen, my thirty-ninth birthday, bawling my eyes out. I was looking down into the depths of my fruit-bowl, where there lurked in the bottom the classic and oh so fucking poignant still life of one leprous banana flanked with two shrivelled blue furred balls that mibbe had once been . . . what . . . plums? . . . peaches? . . . some fucking Sweet Thing That Had Been Left To Rot . . .

Then on came the song you had requested for me: 'Here's
Doctor Hook' and 'If Not You' . . .

DAVIE. Beautiful song, Barbs, you always loved it, doll. It was a
toss up between that and 'Hey, you look wonderful tonight' . . .

*He does the Eric Clapton 'You Put on Your Make Up, Comb
Down Your Long Blonde Hair' number, air guitar and all,
laughing at himself, and swings her round the floor. She
counters with the words of the Doctor Hook hit –*

BARBS. 'Who is going to water my plants?
Who is gonna *patch my pants*?

DAVIE *keeps dancing her and laughing as he joins in.*

DAVIE. 'And who is gonna give me the chance
To feel brand new . . . '

BARBS. 'Who is going to *iron my shirts*?
Who's going to kiss where it hurts?
And who needs a man when he flirts – '

DAVIE. ' – The way I do?'

BARBS. 'Oo–oo if not you–oo . . . Oo if not you.'

Well, I lifted out that poxetten brown banana, seized my
biggest *sabatier* and I sliced the fucker into three, just for
badness, oh, it was long past the edible stage, and I tipped it
into the waste disposal unit and timmed the pair of plums in
after and I whirred it all up and sent it all scooshing to oblivion
shouting out at the radio: 'Well, I'll tell you pal, it fucking
won't be me!'

And now, Davie, you're going to tell me you've Met Someone . . .

DAVIE. I have. And I'm going to be a Daddy!

BARBS. Oh. Oh. Congratulations.

DAVIE. I knew you'd be pleased for me!

BARBS. Course I am, Davie. Who is the lucky girl?

DAVIE. Her name is Colette . . .

BARBS. – And she is twenty-three!

DAVIE. Twenty-two actually. I met her at the Arcade. She was at
the Caledonian University, know, doing an Interior Design
Degree and she came in looking to see what I had in Deco,

because there's been a revival again, Bakelite's back. Well,
I helped her with her degree show . . .

BARBS. You never wanted kids.

DAVIE. Neither did you.

BARBS. She better be nice.

DAVIE. Colette? Oh she's great. We're going to open a shop, get a
wee business going, specialise in retro and good handmade one
offs. Colette's got a great eye . . .

BARBS. Oh, and you're going to be all right with the bank loan?
Because I don't like to piss on your parade, Davie, but, I tell
you, the Banks at the moment are basically being bastards.

DAVIE. Oh, Colette's Dad has got a right few bob, you know, and
her grandmother left her a Trust Fund that she inherited, there,
when she was twenty-one.

BARBS. Well . . . Congratulations, Davie, my darling, what can
I say?

DAVIE. Say you're happy for us.

BARBS. I'm happy for you, Davie. Maybe it'll who knows
happen for me someday, haha . . .

DAVIE. Course it will. *If* it's what you want. You've always – and
I don't mean anything, nothing bar admiration, Barbs, by this –
been totally brilliant at Getting What You Want.

BARBS. Oh good . . .

DAVIE. Because that lawyer guy –

Involuntarily –

BARBS. – Gordon?

DAVIE. Yes, that Gordon twat, him, couple of year back . . . you
did not want *him*, he didn't deserve you.

BARBS. No? No, I did not want him. At least not while his wife
was dying of cancer and he had that boy and girl to bring
through it all, no, I did not want that on my conscience thank
you very much, I was glad when we agreed we wouldn't see
each other any more, fine, but I must admit it did hurt when he
married the Macmillan Nurse . . .

DAVIE. The guy was a tube.

BARBS. The guy was a tube. Who broke my heart. But never mind, time is a great healer etcetera etcetera. At the ratio, I find, of *minimum* two years agony and suffering for one of true love and happiness, but I've done my time, I'm over Gordon.

I no longer love him . . .

Anyway I don't think, these days, it is a Man I want.

DAVIE. No! Hey, you don't mean –

BARBS. No I don't mean! No. Actually what I was planning was to wine you and dine you and seduce you and persuade you we should try again.

DAVIE. You're kidding.

BARBS. Yeah, I'm kidding.

BARBS takes her first swig of the water. Gets up abruptly.

BARBS. Jesus, Davie, this is flat as piss. I'm going to throw it out.

BARBS disappears swiftly offstage kitchen-side with the plastic bottle and both glasses. DAVIE sits back, swivels his neck, gets up, begins to wander round trying – in vain – to see the right place to hang the Startrite Kids. He admits it to himself, calling out to offstage BARBS –

DAVIE. This is wrong.

He shakes his head. Takes it off the other side – bedroomward, bathroomward.

BARBS. (*from offstage*). What . . . ?

DAVIE backs back on without the Startrite poster. He looks as if at a distance to where he's propped it. Decides it's probably not right there either.

DAVIE. I says, I don't think it's gonny fit in, doll.

BARBS. Overheard at a party!

DAVIE. Acht!

DAVIE is not very keen on camp BRENDAN-style remarks. He gives up on the poster too, leaving it there off stage. He goes and looks in towards her in the kitchen, smells the cooking, looks back towards the cutlery set out on the table by the unopened bottle in its bucket. The penny finally dropping.

DAVIE. Barbs, haw, what you doing?

BARBS *re-enters, barefaced, shiny and pink.*

BARBS. Nothing. It was just time I washed off that mask, that's all.

DAVIE. I didny eh realise you'd be cooking . . .

BARBS. Marks and Spencers did.

DAVIE. Only . . . what I was hoping . . . well, I wanted to take you out . . . you know . . . a wee bite . . . and meet Colette.

BARBS. Bring her up!

DAVIE. Don't be daft, no, I was going to take you – she's dying to meet you.

BARBS. And me her. Go get her.

DAVIE. Well, I said I'd meet her down . . . you know that Bar Bargo? Half-sevenish . . .

BARBS. Well go go go.

And, eh, give me half an hour, eh? To put my face and the rest of my clothes on. While I work out some creative way of splitting two chicken breasts stuffed with mushroom in wine sauce into three!

DAVIE. C'mere . . .

He gives her a hug. She pushes him away.

BARBS. Go on!

DAVIE *goes. Looking behind him . . . she's managing to smile. Till he gets out the door at least. Then she's alone with her feelings.*

BARBS *goes to the CD player, puts on Scott Walkers 'No Regrets' then briskly goes to the table, picks up the champagne, icebucket and cutlery dumps it unceremoniously through in the kitchen. She picks up the wedding photograph, glances at it once and takes it off bedroom / bathroomwards comes back immediately with her make up bag. All the while singing along*

with Scott W. On 'No tears goodbye, I don't want you back,
we'd only cry again', she sits down on the sofa, picks up her
makeup bag it and begins to paint a bright red mouth on her
face.

Black.

Music continues as bridge:

Scene Five

Lights come up on BARBS's *empty loft apartment.*

Darkness. Night. Door opens and BARBS *enters talking. With*
GRANT STEEL, *an extremely attractive young man in his early*
to mid twenties, in tow. They are both nervous but both fancy
themselves good at hiding it.

She switches on lights. He looks around, appraising, taking it all
in for, clearly, the very first time.

BARBS. – about eighteen months ago. Well, the flat I had, out
   West – it was a nice flat but I had outgrown it, basically, and I
   knew the architect that was developing this building . . . and
   the idea of a *loft*, designing it by myself for myself, lots of
   space . . .

GRANT. Great! Wow! A bed platform I've always loved these.

She motions him towards the chair.

BARBS. Oh, that's just the guest sleep-space. Drinks . . . ? I'll get
   you a drink. Grant. Sit down. Relax. What would you like?

He sits down considering the single chair then going for the
sofa.

GRANT. What have you got?

   BARBS *goes to the rather well stocked drinks trolley and*
   begins to rummage.

BARBS. Everything. All the usual stuff. I mean, there's vodka, G.
   and T., brandy, correction there's just *about* a cognac left in
   here. There is a very nice, well I don't myself, but my husband
   says this is a very good malt?

GRANT. You're, eh, married then?

BARBS. Separated. Amicably. He's my best friend. One of my best friends.

GRANT. Do you have maybe a beer?

BARBS. Sure . . . I think I've got a couple in the fridge.

She goes to the kitchen to fetch it. He gets up and wanders around, even climbs a step or two of the loft bed steps.

GRANT. Wicked place this . . . !

BARBS *re-enters with a beer by the neck, goes towards him.*

BARBS. Thank you . . . Glass?

GRANT. Bottle.

Seizing all of same, he takes it and pulls her towards him with the other arm and kisses her full on the mouth. She stands back amazed.

BARBS. I'm sorry . . . I think you've got the wrong idea . . .

GRANT. Listen, I should go.

BARBS. No. No. Sit down. Grant. Please . . .

GRANT. I'm sorry . . . I just . . . well, when you asked me up here for a drink –

BARBS. I said for a drink, not 'for coffee'!

GRANT. I apologise. I was way out of line there. Wires crossed.

BARBS. Please. Have a drink. Grant. Relax . . . I'm going to.

Silence. They both drink. An awkward silence. He tries to backtrack.

GRANT. Fantastic space! It must be great to be downtown like this, near all the clubs . . . Merchant City, eh?

BARBS. Merchant City! As my auld mammy calls it, the Back o' Goldbergs.

He looks puzzled.

BARBS, *more rattled than she'd like to let on, starts rabbiting.*

BARBS. Sorry, course you don't know what I'm talking about, you didn't grow up in Glasgow plus you're too young anyway, but Goldbergs, just round the block there, Goldbergs was this big warehouse where you had to get a line for it, you know, you paid things up? Provident cheques, I believe. My mother was a widow so she paid up everything. My brother and I used to get brought into the town twice a year, given a shot up and down the escalator in Lewis's, and taken into Goldbergs – July sales and January – to get kitted out wi school clothes a size too big for us that we'd grow into.

Once they were worn out.

Goldbergs! See Goldbergs, see glamorous! They had this pool, a pond, you know, like sunk in the ground salesfloor with *goldfish* –

GRANT. Samuel Goldwyn's name was Goldfish!

BARBS. Eh . . . ?

GRANT. Samuel Goldfish. Originally. Maybe Goldberg's real name was Goldfish, so –

You know, 'include me out . . . ?' 'let's have some new clichés . . . ?'

BARBS. Right! 'In two words – '

Their eyes meet.

BARBS *and* GRANT. 'Im Possible!'

They smile. Then have to look away from each other. He clears his throat. Silence again.

BARBS. Have you been up here long?

Puzzled, he almost goes to look at his watch.

GRANT. Oh, you mean up in *Glasgow*? Ages. No, not long actually, I suppose. Not that long. Relatively.

I only came up to go to college. A post-graduate thing. Film and TV. But that was a bummer so I left. And I stayed.

BARBS. Right . . .

Silence. He swigs his beer.

BARBS. Listen, Grant, when I met you in that bar last week . . .

GRANT. That wasn't your husband you were with then, was it?

BARBS. No, that was my friend Brendan. And that was his
boyfriend Cammy . . .

GRANT. I thought so.

BARBS. Well, it must've looked like I was picking you up or
something, I do realise that.

GRANT. And you definitely weren't.

I mean, you don't actually, do you, want me to do any
modelling for those pictures for the salon?

BARBS. No – well, at least, I *do*. I think it would be really great
if you did our photo session. I mean, I think you'd be great,
perfect in fact, well, if you fancied it . . . ? And it would be a
bit of pin money –

GRANT. – which would be fine by me. I'm saving like mad at the
moment. To go travelling. Which is why I'm working nights in
that bar anyway.

BARBS. Well, great.

But, you're right. It was . . . a pretext so that I could get –
Grant, when I asked you if you would meet me briefly, tonight,
for a quick drink, there was something else I wanted to talk to
you about. In private. And, och, I suppose it was daft of me to
think I could just meet you quietly across the road for a quick
cappuccino –

GRANT. That bloody woman was all over you like a rash, wasn't
she? Who was she? Really seemed to think you'd changed her
life –

BARBS. – Yup, where actually all I had done was cut off five
inches of bad perm and tired highlights and pluck her
eyebrows. On TV though, so I suppose you can't blame her for
being all obsessed with her five minutes of fame.

GRANT. Sorry?

BARBS. It's just this silly morningtime television thing, it's quite
camp actually, that they've decided to make out of Glasgow.
Seeing as we're your regional style capital of Europe.

GRANT. Are you?

BARBS. Are we buggery, it's all a lot of bollox but am I
complaining? Except when, like tonight, I'm trying to have a

private conversation . . . So, I invited you up here. There was something I wanted to ask you . . .

GRANT. Ask away . . .

BARBS. No. Forget it. Just let's have a quiet drink . . . (*Beat.*)

So you're off round the world then as soon as you get the money together.

GRANT *nods.*

GRANT. Soon as poss . . .

BARBS. Great! I mean, travel. Fantastic. Wish I'd done that at your age. Another beer?

GRANT. I won't thanks.

BARBS *gives herself another slug of vodka.*

BARBS. Music . . . ?

GRANT *shakes his head slowly, looks at her very directly.*

Silence.

GRANT. And there is, unfortunately, no chance you are after my body?

BARBS. No.

GRANT. Number one fantasy bites the dust. Oh well. Cheers.

He takes a long and draining swig of his beer. Looks at her.

GRANT. Shoot.

BARBS. I know your mother.

GRANT. You know my . . . ? Oh, you mean you know *Alice*.

BARBS. Yes.

GRANT. And?

BARBS. And she was telling me you wanted to . . . cool the relationship.

GRANT. And this has exactly what to do with you?

BARBS. It is none of my business, no. But Alice is my friend. She and I, we go way back.

GRANT. And?

BARBS. She is heartbroken. Heart broken. Devastated.

GRANT. And who are you? I mean who exactly the fuck are you?
To try to tell me –

He gets up and picks up his jacket, heads for the door. BARBS
gets between him and it.

BARBS. She is my sister. In law. I married her brother. But that's
irrelevant. Look, she doesn't know anything about me talking
to you like this. She would go apeshit. Don't you dare tell her
I invited you up here!

GRANT. You are a bit of an interfering old cow aren't you?

BARBS. Yes, I am. Yes.

Look, Grant, I knew nothing about your existence till a couple
of months ago. She just . . . all these years. Said nothing.

But, if you had heard how happy she was that you'd tracked
her down . . . She was ecstatic.

Then last week she turns up at the aerobics in bits.

Well, couple of nights later, I'm in that club with Brendan and
Cammy and I spy you behind the bar –

GRANT. How did you know who I was?

BARBS. I saw you together. You and Alice. It must've been your
first meeting.

GRANT. You what?

BARBS. Saw you. Having lunch.

GRANT. What the fuck was going on? You mean she brought you
along to give me the once over from behind the pillars or what?

BARBS. No, no nothing like –

GRANT. This makes me feel . . . spied on, actually. Look, I am
out of here –

BARBS. No. Don't go, please. Not yet. I mean, think about it
from her point of view . . . Alice. She gets pregnant. At the age
of seventeen. These were very different days then, Grant, you
probably wouldn't believe how different . . .

GRANT. Had she never heard of the Pill?

BARBS. Oh, yes, I expect she had! The swinging sixties, all that stuff, they were past and gone already, I expect she'd read the Honey magazine with all the rest of us.

Anyway, she had you, had you adopted and you've had a nice life, haven't you?

GRANT. So so.

BARBS. Legally it is up to the adopted child to get in touch isn't it?

So it was up to you.

Alice said your eighteenth birthday went past, the nineteenth, twentieth . . .

GRANT. I am nearly twenty-six.

BARBS. So what made you do it now?

GRANT. I don't know . . . I . . . wanted to know. (*Beat.*) Did you know my father?

BARBS. I did, actually . . . Though I never knew Alice went out with him.

GRANT. They tell me he was a right evil bastard.

BARBS. Well, I don't know that I'd say evil . . .

GRANT. Stabbed to death in a prison brawl in Barlinnie in 1981. That is quite a thing to find out about your biological parent.

BARBS. I expect it is . . .

GRANT. What was he like?

BARBS. Physically . . . he looked a lot like you, Hannegan. He was very handsome. Famously so, round our scheme.

GRANT. Did you go out with him?

A beat –

BARBS. No.

Alice and he were never an item either. Not openly. Not really. She says when he found out she was pregnant he just did not want to know . . .

GRANT. Bastard, eh?

BARBS. And now, you turn up, the spitting image of him, and then you say you don't want to see her any more.

GRANT. Listen, Barbara . . . I've got a Mum and Dad.

I always knew I had been adopted. 'We chose you because we loved you.' All that.

I didn't say anything to them about looking for my natural parents. I don't know why. I didn't know if I'd get anywhere anyway . . .

Finding Alice, well, it was curiosity. A curiosity satisfied.

And I *liked* her. You couldn't not. I mean, I think my own mother would like her actually . . .

But when I told my Mum about tracking down Alice . . . Well, I felt disloyal, that's what I felt . . .

BARBS. And you feel no need to continue the contact?

GRANT. I'd like to . . . keep in touch.

BARBS. You mean in a Christmas Card sort of a way?

GRANT. Yeah. Why not. Yeah.

Take all this . . . extended family stuff. I can't handle it. Well, Alice has a husband. Fair enough. Great. And daughters. They are my half sisters. By blood anyway. But what I felt about them . . . well they're lovely girls, yeah, but I didn't feel as if I could feel what I felt I was expected to feel.

Which made me feel really shitty.

It was . . . too much . . .

What got to me was this business of Noelene's Eighteenth Birthday party. *I* don't want to go. Noelene certainly doesn't want me to go . . .

So I thought . . . as I am leaving anyway, soon, – I told you I am planning on going to Australia, New Zealand, Japan –

BARBS. But why cut off like that? Break things . . . I mean, if you are leaving anyway, can't you just let it cool down naturally?

Grant, Alice doesn't want anything of you.

GRANT. No? She wants me to be her son. You see the big problem is: to Alice I'm her son. But to me she's not my mother.

BARBS. I will give you some money for your travel fund if you just don't do this to Alice.

He looks long and hard at her as if she is dirt, turns and leaves. The door shuts with a slam behind him.

BARBS *sits on the sofa deeply troubled. Silence. No music.*

Fade to black.

End of Act One.

ACT TWO

Scene One

BRENDAN, *alone in* BARBS*'s livingroom, is looking at an old
'Anniversary of Death of Diana' issue of 'Hello', or something
similar. Facing the audience is a big enough picture of the
Princess to register loud and clear. He turns a page and sighs.*

BRENDAN. Totally tragic . . . And jist when she'd finally got her
hair lukkin haulfwey decent as well . . .

BARBS *comes from the kitchen hands him a glass of red wine.*

BARBS. So what did you think of her?

BRENDAN. – Who? Davie's Colette? She seemed nice enough,
aye!

BARBS *sweeps back into the kitchen.*

BRENDAN. I thought to myself, well, Teenie-fae-Troon, you're
no feart, putting yourself into my hands, swanning in here to
Razor City without an appointment. I thought, see if Barbs had
any *agenda*, or see if she was afflicted with a vindictive nature,
she'd give you Tash and a month of bad herr days . . .

All I done actually, boss, was to do a deep conditioning
and just take the very ends off because she's growing out a
Rachel . . .

Bonny lookin lassie . . . Pleasant to talk to . . . A bit kinna . . .
Kilmal*colm.*

The question is: what does she see in Davie?

I mean, yous vanilla breeders, eh? Whit like urr ye? A closed
book tae me . . .

Smells great. Spicy, eh? Cammy will be pleased. More Tastier
Snax Later . . . Marinade me . . .

Want any help?

BARBS *calls from kitchen.*

BARBS. Nope!

BRENDAN. OK, I'll put oan some music. If I can find anything. Your taste is in your arse, no your ears!

He begins to look through a pile of old vinyl, holding up a vintage Sinatra, a Nat King Cole, not fancying any of it. He continues calling out to her offstage –

BRENDAN. Anyway what I really wanted to tell you: And I have talked it over with Cammy, because, obviously, he's my partner, right? It affects him if I decide to take on a parenting role . . .

Well, I've not said anything up till now, well obviously I've thought a lot about it ever since your birthday, ever since that night you asked us –

And yes . . . well, when it came down to it . . . Ach, Barbsie, I don't want you to think I was one of those Big-Void-In-My-Life Queens with the strong maternal instinct girning on about their secret sadness. Because I don't honestly think I was.

BARBS *enters, her eyes like saucers. Stands there.*

BRENDAN. But I thought to myself: Yes I *would* like to have a baby.

Correction I'd like to have Barbs's baby. If – and only if – I can have a continuing . . . presence . . . in that baby's life. A connection. Commitment. Of some sort.

So Cammy's attitude was: it's up to me.

Well I know I've been a while getting back to you on this one, but obviously I had to have an AIDS test – oh, I can see it on your face, you never thought of that, did you Barbs, you never thought it through, you just came out with it and asked me, the question expecting the answer No . . . I had to have the Test. And Cammy had to have the Test.

It is a thought to do it. Because obviously the best way to live your life is to assume you're not but everybody else could be, so practise safe sex anyway. And I have been practising. I'm even getting quite good at it . . . But anyway me 'n' Cammy, we decided: This is the Start of Our Relationship, it's *serious* we want this to work out, we'll both go and Get Tested.

Well obviously it takes a wee while. For the results. And to be sure . . .

But it was fine. We are both free from H.I.V.

So do you know what this is? Correct. Useful Utensil Number Sixty-Nine. A. Turkey. Baster. (Naw, I'd never seen wan either I'd *wondered* what like it was.) This mother is meant to put that magic elixir, that 10 c.c., that lovin' spoonful up therr wherr the sun don't shine . . .

Listen, Barbs Marshall, hey, don't you dare kid on that night you were only kidding on because you wereny, I know you wereny. Say Yes. Yes I would like us to try for a baby. Say it!

BARBS *opens her mouth and shuts it again. She rushes into his arms. They embrace.*

Black.

Music bridge. Billy Swann's 'If You Got a Problem (Don't care what it is / I can help / I got two strong arms/ Let me help / It would sure do me good to do you good / Let me help' . . .).

Scene Two

One single exciting, eyecatching and beautiful designer Christmas decoration, perhaps fairy-lit, on the table tells the audience it's coming on Christmas.

BARBS *is lying on the floor with her legs up.* BRENDAN *sits on the couch painting her toenails with nail varnish.*

BRENDAN. How long do you have to keep your feet up?

BARBS. Lot longer than it'll take that to dry anyway.

BRENDAN. Wonder if it'll work this time?

BARBS. Time will tell . . .

BRENDAN. How do you feel?

BARBS. Pregnant.

BRENDAN. Do you?

BARBS. No. Not yet. Did you wash out the middleman?

BRENDAN. Sappled it through in waarm soapy watter, dried it
aff, and put it by in your bathroom cabinet for the next shot.

BARBS. Brendan, this might take a wee while to work. I mean
your auld Auntie Barbara isny as young as she used to be.

BRENDAN. By the way, this nail varnish is gonny take three
coats an' all . . .

BARBS. At this point in time, Brendan, if we have done it right,
there are more than two hundred million motile sperm
currently swimming up my fanny towards The One And Only
out of my dwindling supply of my somewhat elderly eggs
which has hopefully ripened, travelled along the clagged up old
fallopian plumbing and got itself into position for
the moonshot. I mean two hundred million. Constantly
replenishing themselves. To one. Out of a finite number that
were there since before the day I was born female.

Two hundred million. To one. That's not equal. How can we
say men and women are the same or ever could be?

I mean, Brendan, *you*, you bastard, are – and this is you till
you're ninety – just sitting there manufacturing more sperm to
replace the two hundred million you just flang away.

BRENDAN. Huv you been reading books again? Actually I didny
find it aw that easy to manage my Wee Fling to tell you the
truth . . .

BARBS. How come?

BRENDAN. That was the question . . . ! Och, I'm shy, Hairy
Melon, I'm shy . . .

BARBS. Canny get aff in a lassie's bedroom, is that the trouble?

BRENDAN. Nor in thon designer bathroom of yours neither
without giving myself a severe talking to. And normally I've
only got to smell the *paper* of Farm Boys in Gingham and
that's me. Faster than shite aff a shovel. Tellin' you Barbsie, if
it's all the same with you – *if* we've got to try again next month
– I'll produce it at home and bring it round like we did last
month, OK?

BARBS. 'S up to yourself . . . Enlist the help of Cammy for all
I care. Just as long as you hotfoot it round here with the
product . . .

BRENDAN. When will you know?

BARBS. I'll keep you posted. (*Beat.*) Away down and get us both
some Haagen-Dazs, go an', it's E.R. night. The Deli downstairs
is still open, you'll just catch it. Take my keys, they're on the
table, I'm no about to get up and open the door to you, am I?

BRENDAN. Don't say I'm not – extremely – good to you.

The phone rings. And rings.

BARBS. Shit, the machine's not on. Give us it over.

BRENDAN. Belgian Chocolate?

She lifts the receiver.

BARBS. Hello? Hello Stranger! (*To* BRENDAN.) Cookie Dough!

BRENDAN *leaves waving keys.*

BARBS. No, I was talking to somebody else . . . It's OK he's just
going. Well, well Wee Bro, how's things?

*She listens swivelling her ankles and surveying her bonny red
toenails.*

BARBS. Me? Oh fine and dandy, right now. Totally . . . laid back.

Well of course we're busy, yeah, right through Christmas up till
the New Year. All go.

Ninety what? I don't want to hear it. Here it's the dreich, dark,
days of Glesca in December, remember?

Mmhm. Mmhm. Oh Ma is fine. She is the same as ever. She's
indestructible. Indefensible most of the time, but och aye, just
the same. She's taken up aromatherapy, her and Mina. Up the
community centre. Had to shell out a fortune for her Basic Kit
so here's hoping she sticks in at it.

Last Thursday, Yup same as ever. Shake-and-vacced the
shagpile then advanced on my pressure points with neroli oil
and lavender. Set my teeth on edge and all my nerve ends a-
jangle but then that's likely just me . . .

The downstairs buzzer goes. She covers the receiver.

BARBS. Come in Brendan you daft bastard you've got the keys!
(*Back to* BILLY *and the phone call.*) Sorry. Christmas? Ma's.
I did ask her here, but no joy. It is the duty of every singleton,

divorcee and sadfuck to pack their fluffy pyjamas and allow themselves to be sucked back into the bosom of the parental home for a threeday torporfest.

Listens. A smile begins to spread across her face.

BARBS. You're on! She would come, she would, if I came too. Why not? Next Christmas. Yes! Australia! Christmas day on a beach for once in my life. This time next year . . .

She looks down at her hands cupping her flat belly. Crosses fingers.

BARBS. Who knows . . . ? We'll *all* come . . . I'll just book the tickets and surprise her. Yeah . . . We'll do it. Let Ma spend some perfect time with all her grandchildren . . .

The door opens and SADIE *enters with her key and a shopping bag and a plastic bag too.*

BARBS *is of course unable to see who has come in –*

BARBS. Hi Brendan!

SADIE. What you daen, Barbara, I rang the buzzer but nae answer . . .

BARBS. Mum! I'm just on the phone to our Billy. Do you want a wee word . . . ?

SADIE. No thanks. I spoke to him last night. Tell him no to waste money on the phone.

BARBS. Billy, I'll phone you back later, Bills, all right? Time is it there anyway? OK.

She hangs up.

SADIE. What the hell are you daen lying on your back like that. Have you slipped a disc?

BARBS. No.

SADIE. Well get up, you dizzy article, the back of your jumper will get aw oose.

BARBS *gets up.*

BARBS. Ma, what are you doing here?

From out of the plastic bag, SADIE *sets a light up novelty talking Christmas tree on the table. Shoving* BARBS's *decor aside.*

SADIE. Look what they were selling in Argyle Street, I was in doing ma latenite Christmas shopping. Cheery intit? I thought to myself oor Barbs does a lot of enter*tain*ing . . .

The tree winks and blinks and says 'Merry Christmas, Ho Ho Ho.'

BARBS *looks at it amazed.* SADIE *with delighted triumph.*

SADIE. Well, I wisny going to humph it all the way home on the bus and humph it all the way back in here on Thursday. I thought to myself I'll pop up.

BARBS. And you're very welcome. My pal Brendan – you remember Brendan?

SADIE. Aye, him that's right yon wey? Nice enough laddie . . .

BARBS. He's great! Well he'll be back up in a minute. He's away for icecream. The three of us could have a bowl of icecream and watch the telly together. E.R.'s on later. You know, with Him You Like? Away through and get three bowls and some spoons . . .

SADIE *exits kitchenward,* BARBS *following her.*

BRENDAN *enters with his key and two tubs of Haagen-Daz. Shouting loudly as he comes in.*

BRENDAN. Pralines 'n' Cream and Belgian Chocolate. Quickie-quick because that George Clooney is *such* a shag!

BARBS *shoots out of the kitchen pantomiming frantically for him to shut up.*

BRENDAN. What the fuck are you doing on your pins, Mrs, because you'll be *spilling*!

Behind him SADIE *re-enters with bowls and spoons.* BRENDAN*'s attention is fixated on the talking Christmas tree.*

BRENDAN. Knock ma pan in wanking out hardwon spunk for you to just let scale down your silken thighs and go to w – what the *fuck* is that?

BARBS. It's a present. From my mum here.

SADIE. Hello Brendan.

BRENDAN. Mrs. Kirkwood! Sadie . . . !

BARBS. Mum, siddown . . .

SADIE. I think I'll maybe better get up the road . . .

BARBS. Not at all, Mother, sit down, please.

SADIE. I'll see you Thursday, pet, same as usual . . .

BARBS. Mother, Brendan and I have Just Been Making Babies.

SADIE *looks from one to the other astonished. Appalled.*

BRENDAN. Yes, well, time for a quick sharp exit . . .

BRENDAN *goes and gets his jacket from the peg.*

BARBS. – Hopefully. We hope to get me pregnant. Don't we Brendan?

BRENDAN. Barbs, I think you and your Ma need a wee –

BARBS. Sit down Brendan. Sit down Mother.

SADIE. You're only doing this to upset me!

BARBS *laughs.*

BARBS. Ha! No, – and I do go to great lengths for you Mother, granted – but strangely enough I'm doing this to make me happy.

SADIE. What about the child? And anyway what do you think children have to do with happiness?

BARBS. Ach, here we go!

SADIE. All you had to do was ask me!

BARBS. Ah yes. And I know what you'd've said. 'I was a widow by the time I was thirty –

SADIE. I was. And you and Billy had my heart roasted.

BARBS. Mother, you don't mean that.

SADIE. By God and I do. Disgusting! That's what it is. He's a bloody homosexual! You can't –

BRENDAN. It isny hereditary, Mrs. Kirkwood. Obviously. Work it out. I mean, think about it.

Sadie, eh, we didn't actually –

BARBS. That is none of her business!

SADIE. With a test tube! That's hellish! It's perverted! Plus AIDS. Think of that.

BARBS. Ah, Brendan, we are talking to the biggest bigot in the West here. You are in the presence of the woman who went in the huff, went *in the huff* with our dog Trooper when she caught him humping Blackie, Mrs Bain's big butch labrador up Hinshelwood Quadrant . In the huff. With a dug!

SADIE. No harm to you, Brendan, but to me it's not and never will be natural.

BRENDAN. Listen, I'm away, Barbara. You and your Ma have some talking to do. In private.

BARBS. Don't you dare go anywhere!

BRENDAN. Barbs, darlin', you want me phone me later. Night, Mrs. Kirkwood, Nice Christmas and, eh, All the Best When it Comes . . .

BRENDAN *exits. Depositing her keys on the table.*

SADIE. You just don't know what to be at!

BARBS. On the contrary I have never actually been so one hundred percent clear about what I want.

SADIE. Stupid. You think you are so bloody smart but you do not have a clue. Dream World, that's what you live in. Selfish. Selfish to the core. Think it is a joke to bring up a child on your own?

BARBS. No. No I don't. You did it. You did it well. For two of us. We turned out all right, me and our Billy.

SADIE *makes a noise of disgust and scorn.*

BARBS. Say it. Say we turned out OK. Say it!

SADIE. I don't know you. Either of the bloody two of you.

BARBS. You did it. You did it all by yourself!

SADIE. And what choice did I have? Do you think I'd have chosen that for my life?

And you want to *deliberately* . . . Ach!

Well, I will tell you one thing, I won't be up here babysitting, bailing you out, the same as I've done with everything else.

Once the novelty wears off and you want your life back and your freedom back don't think I'll be here watching it and loving it and helping you out because I won't.

BARBS. Mum, I am nearly forty. Mum, my life is not your life. Mammy, please don't go in the huff.

SADIE does. She goes, takes her present and leaves. BARBS is alone, distraught.

The bell goes.

BARBS. Thank Christ!

She throws open the door. To GRANT.

BARBS. Oh!

GRANT. I've just been out with Alice. Having a drink.

BARBS. Oh.

GRANT. We talked and stuff. I just thought you'd want to know. I mean I was pissed off at the time. But I thought, later, you know . . . About what you said. I mean, you're right, she's not nothing to me. I thought I should tell you. The outside door was open. Sorry, I should have buzzed. Have I come at a bad time?

BARBS. Bad time, good time, who knows . . . Come on in anyway.

Black.

Music bridge: the Loving Spoonful's 'Darling Be Home Soon.'

Scene Three

It is Valentine's Day almost two months later.

On the table are a single red rose in a tall vase and a large card which is just a big red heart on silver.

Lights come up on BARBS and GRANT, post shower, she's in a huge white fluffy robe, he's in Calvin Klein underpants. She's on the sofa, he's on the floor, she's towelling his wet hair, he's reading to himself the sleevenotes on the album cover. It's that present DAVIE gave her months ago. The Lovin' Spoonful LP.

The song ends ('For the great relief of having you to talk to . . . ') and it clicks off.

GRANT. Hey listen to this! I love it! . . . 'The car radio suddenly burst into "Do You Believe in Magic" which is how I met the Lovin' Spoonful . . . First they were only a name and that great song so immediately touching, so perfect in its presence . . . Despite the song they had trouble believing in the magic of rock and roll When The Rock and Roll Was Them.'

Brilliant! Where do you get this stuff?

BARBS *swipes away the album cover.*

BARBS. Never mind. It's old!

GRANT. Can I have it?

BARBS. I'll make you a tape.

GRANT. Just a loan of?

BARBS. I'll tape it for you. With all the other golden oldies you're so keen on. You better hurry up, you're late for your work already.

GRANT. Maybe I won't go. It is Valentine's after all. Surely all the goodtime people will be staying home tonight like what we did. Like what we do all the time, Barbarella.

BARBS. Don't start that again!

GRANT. Well is there something wrong with wanting to go out with you? In Public. My flatmates don't believe you're real. C'mon, let your hair down, Rapunzel. Why can't we go to the movies – ?

BARBS. What's wrong with staying home with the Classic Video Collection.

GRANT. Nothing. You know I love the Classic Video Collection. *Schwee*theart.

BARBS. Well then. Away and work!

GRANT. Can I come up after I finish? I'll promise not to wake you.

BARBS. Hah!

GRANT. Well, there's a first time for everything . . .

BARBS. Hey! I wasn't complaining . . .

GRANT. I should think not.

BARBS. Not even a toty wee bit. Do you want a sandwich before you go?

GRANT. Here's yet another way I'm good for you! Before you met me your fridge was full of make up. Now there's Real Food, bacon and bagels and everything –

BARBS. Well you are a growing boy.

GRANT. – and yogurt with wheatgerm . . .

BARBS. – and I need all my strength to keep up with you, don't I?

They kiss.

GRANT. C'mere!

He takes her over to the bottom of the steps up to the loft bed.

GRANT. Well, you know we've made love just about everywhere in this apartment? We've had the snogs on the sofa, the knee-tremblers in the shower and the table-enders in the kitchen, not to speak of all the lay-lady-lays across your big brass bed . . .

BARBS. So?

GRANT. One place we've never done it is up in the loft bed here. And I've always wanted to.

BARBS. So?

GRANT. We're going to. I'm going to put on this hippy music, and we'll smoke a joint and we'll make long slow summer of love hippy love . . .

BARBS. Hey, what age do you think I am? Oh God, Grant, I don't think I've smoked a joint since the Tories got into power . . .

GRANT puts on the music. The sound of the Lovin' Spoonful fills the room again. This time it is 'The Full Measure'. GRANT goes over to the couch and takes a packet of Rizlas and a tin out of his jeans pocket, singing and jiving away.

BARBS. One sec. Bathroom. One sec.

BARBS disappears bathroomwards and GRANT still dancing climbs up into the loft bed space. He takes out a rolled joint, lights it, inhales. Looks down over the edge. BARBS reappears. GRANT *throws those white underpants at her. She ducks then picks them up –*

GRANT. Hey, Marshall, get your gorgeous ass up here.

– And BARBS *clowns around flashing at him and dancing and singing along to ' . . . Wonderful feeling / Could it be someone's telling me – AAAH! / I know that you know the feeling / That something for nothing is wrong / Getting love is so easy / Giving love takes so long . . . '*

Suddenly the inside *doorbell goes and the letter box is raised and rattled.*

ALICE*'s eyes peek through. Very loudly –*

ALICE. Haw! Haw, Barbara, open the door will you? It's me. Alice.

BARBS. Christ!

BARBS *runs back to the wall by the door, flattens herself against it, panicking.* GRANT *leans over the loft signalling at her to ignore it. She crawls under the letterbox on the door, trying ludicrously to keep out of sight and puts the music up louder. Crawls back, waving up at* GRANT *to stay there. It's a ridiculous routine only stopped by* ALICE *shouting through again.*

ALICE. I know you're there, open up?

BARBS *waves at* GRANT *to keep out of sight and, giving up opens the door.* ALICE *comes in, invited or not.*

ALICE. Christ that music's deafening!

BARBS. Sorry . . .

BARBS *swiches off the music.*

ALICE. Are you . . . on your own?

BARBS. Yeah! Sometimes I'm in myself I just like to play old records really loud . . . !

ALICE. Aye well, that's three weeks in a row you've missed the aerobics. (*Beat.*) Have you been smoking dope?

BARBS. I've been really busy. (Dope, please, no since I split up wi Davie!) Awfy busy! Work stuff. Well not tonight, obviously. Shaving my legs. How did you get in here?

ALICE. You opened the door . . .

BARBS. Naw I mean into the building. Is the entrance lock buggered again?

ALICE. Not as far as I know. Somebody came out just as I arrived and I asked them to hold open the door for me. I didny want to buzz up and have you no answer.

BARBS. Why wouldn't I answer?

BARBS *suddenly realises she's holding the underpants and looks at them with horror before stuffing them into her pocket. Alice does not register this though.*

ALICE. I asked Brendan, he says the same. You never go out with him and Whatsisname any more. He's worried about you.

BARBS. Is he stuff!

ALICE. Have you gone agoraphobic? Or what? Hey, check the –

BARBS. I'm fine!

ALICE. – Valentine! And a single red rose! Do tell!

BARBS. Nothing *to* tell. Stefan gave every girl at work one. Probably cynically meant but you know me, I'll refuse nothing but blows. And a rose is a rose is a rose. And the Valentine –

BARBS *opens and shuts the card to reveal that it says* ALL *my love and is signed '?'*

BARBS. – Doesny say! Traditional eh no? No, it was actually the wan wi a bit of taste from the fanmail sack at the programme this morning. I couldny resist bringing it back to cheer myself up. Sad eh?

ALICE. Some poor sucker went to the bother of making this imagine! For a total stranger?

BARBS. Tele's weird.

ALICE. Even Buns of Steel was asking for you.

BARBS. What did she say?

ALICE. Said she'd thought she was a good judge of character after all these years as an aerobics instructor and she hadn't taken you for a backslider. Told me to remind you to make sure you kept up the pelvic thrusts.

BARBS. Jesus . . .

ALICE. Anyway I haveny seen you since Noelene's Eighteenth.
What did you think of it? I thought it was quite a nice night.

BARBS. A smashing night Alice. And Noelene looked gorgeous.

ALICE. Thanks to the swanky haircut.

BARBS. Brendan's very good.

ALICE. She's a lucky lucky girl. I says to her I hope your Auntie
Barbara knows you appreciate her. Anyway, did you get to
meet Grant? What did you think?

BARBS. He seemed . . . a nice boy.

ALICE. I hope so. I want him to be happy Barbara.

BARBS *tries to get* ALICE *to the door and out.*

BARBS. I know . . . Anyway, Alice dear heart, why don't I take
you out for lunch –

ALICE. What I really wanted to ask you was: did you phone your
mother yet?

BARBS. I don't want to talk about it!

Alice, she went in the huff with me, she should be the one –
Ach, I will. I will do, O.K? Alice, why can't she treat me like a
human being and no like 'her daughter'.

ALICE. Because you *are* her daughter. But phone her, eh?
Because I saw her on Sunday there when I was in The Place
visiting my ma.

BARBS. Eh?

ALICE. No! No! She was in visiting. With her pal Mina visiting
an old lady they had been in the church club with or
something.

BARBS. How was she?

ALICE. Oh, fine, fine. She's very sparky your Ma. Wonderful
appearance too when she's done up.

BARBS. She's not old, Alice.

ALICE. Neither she is. Unlike mines.

BARBS. How is she?

ALICE. Dear oh dear oh dear.

Ach you have to laugh sometimes. It can be quite funny. Some of what she comes out with, you know. Doesn't know me! At least your mother has all her marbles.

BARBS. Hah!

ALICE. She does. You're lucky! Your Ma can be very funny! *Intentionally* funny! She told me a joke. In The Place on Sunday there, that wan of the orderlies tellt her: What's sixty feet long and smells of pish? A conga line in an old folk's home!

BARBS. Christ!

ALICE. She has a sense of humour, Barbs, sometimes I think you just don't appreciate it.

BARBS. Obviously not overburdened with empathy for the poor old terminally bewildered . . .

ALICE. Ach, Barbs, she's no old yet! Plus you do have to laugh. (*Beat.*) Look, I know she really offended you saying what she said about Brendan – and ach, I know you are probably waiting for a result before –

BARBS. I said I really really don't want to talk about it!

With the hot bit of the roach catching the back of his throat, GRANT coughs unwittingly. BARBS coughs, trying to cover it up. Alice finally catches on. She pantomimes 'is somebody up there?' BARBS – eventually – nods. ALICE pantomimes 'Who?' Barbs pantomimes back 'BRENDAN'. Alice repeat pantomimes 'Brendan?' and, realising what he must be there for, pantomimes wanking. Loudly –

ALICE. Jeez oh, Barbs is that the time? Jings, I'll better away. Tommy says he'd pick me up the back of nine . . . Anyway, Barbs, I'll phone you, we'll have our lunch and a good blether, eh? (I'm *so* sorry!)

And she's away. The letter box rises again.

ALICE. Oh, and Phone Your Mother.

BARBS just stands there wating for GRANT to come down. She takes the underpants out of her pocket and tosses them up to the silence of the loft bed.

*Pulling on the pants he descends the staircase, then, unsmiling
and unspeaking, he goes to the bedroom, fetches his clothes
brings them back and puts them on.*

BARBS. Don't say anything!

GRANT. I'm saying nothing!

BARBS. I will tell her! Honestly, I will. When the time is right . . .

GRANT. I almost came down. Bollock naked as I was I nearly
came down. But it's not for me to tell her, is it? I want you to
tell her. I want us to tell her *together* . . . How did you think I
felt up stuck up there like Jesus Christ being denied thrice?
Stefan gave you my rose. The Valentine was from a fucking
fan. I am a nice boy.

Hey! Who the fuck did she think I was anyway?

BARBS. Nobody!

GRANT. Nobody?

BARBS. Just . . . somebody.

GRANT. Why did you let her in?

BARBS. She knew I was here!

GRANT. I tell you, Barbara, I aint gonna put up with this shit
forever.

BARBS. I know . . . Will I see you later? I'll sleep up there and
you can come and surprise me.

GRANT. Surprise you I fuck off home to my own bed for once.

BARBS. You wouldny . . .

GRANT. 'Naw, I wouldny.' (*He kisses her once then smiles.*)
I suppose.

*He goes. She leans against the door shaking her head. Aargh.
After a moment the (outside) buzzer goes. She jumps, then puts
record off, goes to the intercom.*

BARBS. Hello?

BRENDAN. It's me!

BARBS. Brendan?

BRENDAN. Have you forgot what day it is?

BARBS. No! (*Beat.*) I had! Come in, darlin'. Come on up! Perfect!

Music starts: Frank Sinatra singing 'My Funny Valentine'. The doorbell goes. BARBS opens it. BRENDAN sticks out his arm, a little brownbagged parcel in his hand. After 'Sweet comic Valentine – '

BRENDAN. Pro-duct!

Black.

Music bridge continues.

Scene Four

Lights up on BARBS's livingroom.

DAVIE *stands with an empty whisky glass, looking down into it.*

Standing apart from him, holding a full glass absently, not drinking it is BRENDAN. Both men have black ties, sober dark clothes, funeral smart.

ALICE *is there too, wearing her good dark coat, open, over dark dress and stockings. Everyone edgy, isolated from each other.*

BRENDAN. Barbs OK, Alice?

ALICE. I think so. She'll be out in a wee minute, Brendan. I think she wanted, you know, to get changed . . .

BRENDAN *nods, looks towards the bedroom.*

DAVIE *goes and pours himself another large whisky.*

ALICE. Davie, don't you be drinking too much!

DAVIE *glowers at her, advances to BRENDAN with the bottle.*

DAVIE. Brendan! See's your glass . . .

BRENDAN *puts his hand over his glass, shakes his head as GRANT, in white shirt, dark jacket and black tie, comes out of the kitchen with a huge bunch of funeral lilies in an impressive glass vase. He puts them down on the table.*

ALICE. Beautiful son . . .

She indicates the door.

ALICE. On you go too, Grant, if you want. The girls are just away. Andrea's exhausted. She's upset. She's never been to a funeral before. I says, I'll say bye for you to your Auntie Barbs, she'll be awful glad you came, 'preciate it . . . Run, you'll catch them. You can go up the road with the girls.

GRANT. No it's all right, Alice, I'll stay a little while.

DAVIE *glowers at him. He doesn't see it, but* ALICE *does. She glowers back in a warning way.*

ALICE. Thanks, son . . . (*She reads the card which was with the flowers.*) . . . With deepest sympathy from Tiffany, Natasha, Stefan and all at Razor City. Our Barbara, well, she has a lot of good friends there is no doubt about it. But there is nothing – nothing on earth – which can ever make up for losing your mother . . .

BRENDAN. One helluva shock.

ALICE. I know, I know, it's very hard to take in.

DAVIE. *Sadie* . . . unbelievable . . . She was some Sadie . . .

ALICE. That minister did very well with his speech didn't he?

DAVIE *glowers at her again. She takes his point.*

ALICE. I can't believe I just came out with that!

GRANT *exits again towards the bedroom.* DAVIE *glowers after him.*

DAVIE. Fuck's *he* daen' here?

ALICE. Leave him alone, Davie, he just came to support me. It was very good of him.

Ach, it's just terrible. Out of the blue like that. Hellish. Never a day's illness in her life.

BRENDAN. No warning at all, eh?

ALICE. None. No, her old neighbour said the pair of them had been up the community centre the night before and she was the same as ever.

BRENDAN. That's sore. I just hope Barbs'll be OK . . . She'd never made up with Sadie, had she?

DAVIE. What the fuck did they fight about anyway? Sadie and
   Barbs, there was always these wee spats and that, but,
   basically, the two of them were *like that*. I never heard of such
   a thing as them no speaking for three months.

BRENDAN. I know she'd bought her something for Mother's
   Day. She said she was going to go round with a bunch of
   flowers –

ALICE. I know, son, she told me . . .

   When I was up there at the house with Barbs . . . you know,
   day it happened . . . ? And I was looking in cupboards to see if
   we could find anything . . . Like a will or anything. And thae
   cupboards were chocabloc jampacked wi things Barbs gave
   her. Still in their wrapping paper the most of them. Untouched.
   (*Beat.*) Perfume. Silk scarves . . .

BRENDAN. Tragic eh . . . ?

DAVIE. Where's Billy?

ALICE. Where's Billy Kirkwood? Barbs said he's away with that
   couple of friends of his.

DAVIE. That bugger's never around when he's needed . . .

ALICE. Och, Davie, wheesht don't you be causing trouble on a
   day like the day.

DAVIE. Well, bastard fucks off to Australia leaving Barbs to carry
   the whole can with Sadie.

ALICE. Now, now, that's not what Barbs thinks. Plus he was great
   at keeping in touch. He had her out there visiting.

DAVIE. Aye, comes home for the funeral once we've got
   everything arranged and starts putting in his tuppenceworth.
   The minute the sitdown tea's done he just buggers off –

ALICE. Davie, Barbs was pleased he was getting the chance to
   see his friends. It was nice of them to come. Nice looking
   couple.

BRENDAN. Them in the Saab?

ALICE. As well if Billy gets a wee drink and a chance to relax wi
   his pals because it'll have been a right sorrowful homecoming
   for him. That long flight with a heartache at the end of it.

BRENDAN. I think I'll go through and put the kettle on. Barbs'll mibbe just prefer a wee cup of tea.

BRENDAN *exits kitchenward with his whisky glass.*

ALICE. Och, the endless cups of tea, eh? That's what I remember about the time, endless time it seemed, between my Dad going, eh, and the funeral. All the neighbours, mind, Davie? Coming in with cakes and baking . . . A sour mouth and dry sponge cake and gallons of hot sweet tea.

It was awful good you helped Barbs with all the arrangements and everything.

DAVIE. Who else was gonny dae it? I'm still her husband after all.

ALICE. Davie, can I ask you something? Do you and Barbs ever still . . .

DAVIE. What? Get thegether? Like . . . ? Naw. No recently, anyway. Whiles, when we were first split, or yon time she was really upset ower yon lawyer eejit we used to . . . Thing is, Alice, Barbara stopped fancying me, it's as simple as that.

ALICE. Then you wereny lying up there on that bed up there smoking a joint on Valentine's Day?

DAVIE. Me? Not guilty, naw. How?

ALICE *shrugs. Says nothing.*

DAVIE. Christ! What's that bliddy Brendan hinging aboot here for? Does it never occur to emdy Barbra'll be exhausted after a day like the day? Certain times are for family. Know what I mean?

ALICE. Davie, he's her best pal. A big help to her. In many ways that you know nothing about. Can you no just wheesht about things you know nothing about?

DAVIE. Some folk cling on to Barbara – I've told her this – looking for all they can get.

And where's that big gink, Grant? He doesny even know Barbs!

ALICE. He's met her. He met her at Noelene's eighteenth. He's doing no harm Davie.

DAVIE. I says to Colette to no bother coming. She sent a card.

ALICE. He makes me happy, Davie, to see that he turned out all right.

DAVIE. He's curious about you, you're curious about him, fine . . . But then can he no just bugger off?

ALICE. Do you think my Da knew?

I often think, Ma and I, who were we fooling. And for what?

DAVIE. Different days, Alice.

ALICE. Did you not guess, Davie?

DAVIE. I was only about fourteen year aul'. I was just a daft boy.

ALICE. I was just a daft girl.

DAVIE. Could you no have kept it? If you wanted? I mean my Da was strict. But he would've come round. Like everybody else does.

ALICE. I didn't want a baby. I wanted a life.

DAVIE. You could've got an abortion.

ALICE. I went as far as the wummin's close. Cat's pish and cabbage. Then I phoned that number. Hah! There was this advert. 'Pregnant? And don't want to be?' I thought it was an abortion advisory service . . . Pro lifers. They put the fear of death into me!

Ach, I just did what girls in my situation have always done, which is pretend it wasn't happening to me until it was too late and I had to tell my mammy. Oh, she gets me away to the Church of Scotland home in the Highlands, all that, keeps it a big secret from you, a big secret from my Da. Which I doubt. But in those days . . .

Anyway. Nothing Was Ever Said.

I've been thinking a lot about them. The last few days. My ma and my da . . .

DAVIE. I know what you mean. What wi' Sadie . . . Makes you look back. On the past, like, know? Ach, I really, literally, can't take it in. You feel that helpless. For Barbara.

ALICE. There's Our Ma . . . in yon place. Like that. And then there's Sadie . . .

DAVIE. Aye. She was one helluva gal, Old Sadie. Like mother, like daughter.

ALICE. Could Colette no have come today? No, maybe you're right enough that wouldny have been right . . . ?

DAVIE. I didny think so.

ALICE. They get on though, her and Barbs?

DAVIE. Oh, aye, well enough . . . though I think Colette is that wee bit jealous of Barbs, know what I mean?

ALICE. Yeah . . .

DAVIE. Alice, Colette had a termination.

ALICE. Oh no, Davie, and you were that excited.

ALICE *goes towards her brother. Touches his arm.*

ALICE. Was there . . . something wrong? With the baby?

DAVIE. No, no. (*Beat.*) No, Colette decided to listen to her mother and father and all their stuff about her having her whole life in front of her. They booked her into a private clinic. Six weeks ago. It was getting near the cut off point, know?

I was not consulted. I got presented with a fait accompli . . . We've not split up, nor nothing. No, as Colette says, her and me, we've got all the time in the world.

BRENDAN *re-enters with a set tea tray, puts it down.*

BRENDAN. I put out this cake. Likely nobody hungry, but ocht . . .

BARBS *enters with the awful Scene One jersey her mother gave her over her sober black skirt and funeral shoes.*

BARBS. Anybody want a drink?

Beautiful flowers . . .

The minister did well.

ALICE. I was just saying that. Very moving.

GRANT *re-enters and goes up to* BARBS *tries to put his arm around her.*

GRANT. Barbs, don't just walk away from me.

BARBS. Grant, sit down and have a drink, please.

DAVIE. Don't you be upsetting my Barbs on a day like today. What exactly are you on pal?

ALICE. Davie, shut up!

GRANT. Barbara, I want you to tell them who I am.

BARBS. This is Alice's son, Grant Steel. Grant, I think you know everyone with the possible exception of Brendan Boyle.

BRENDAN. I know him. He is the model for the Spring photoshoot.

GRANT. I am in love with Barbara Marshall. She is my lover. Tell them Barbs.

BARBS. I have been having a relationship with this . . . young man.

Alice –

ALICE. Don't touch me!

GRANT. I want you to tell them. Tell them you're in love with me.

BARBS. Grant, please. My mother is dead and I don't know how I am going to live without her.

GRANT. Let me comfort you.

You know I am in love with you and you know how sick I am of being your dirty secret for some reason.

Gets nothing, so has to appeal to ALICE *for help.*

GRANT. I was here, Alice, on Valentine's Day but –

ALICE. You?

GRANT. I wanted to tell you –

Back to BARBS.

GRANT. Why not? I told you, Barbs. I want to go out with you. Oh, staying in with you is all very lovely. This Christmas, yeah, it was the best Christmas of my life. For you too, Barbs you know it was. Say it! Say it.

Silence. She won't. He keeps trying. Won't give up.

GRANT. But I want to go *out* with you. I want you to come to my seedy flat and meet my – actually it's not seedy, I am going to pack in all this apologising for myself.

I am a grown up man of twenty-six and I am in love with you, Barbara.

Is there something strange in that. Am I missing something?

I want to go to the movies with you, eat dinner in public. And I'm never – never – going to be in the position again, Barbs, where I am at Noelene's eighteenth birthday party and you are at Noelene's eighteenth birthday party but I am not even allowed to dance with you. Never again.

Why are you ashamed of me?

Today – today of all days, I want you to tell all them you are in love with me.

BRENDAN. Have you been shagging somebody else while we were trying to have a baby?

GRANT. While you what?

BARBS. I want you all to go away and leave me alone.

GRANT. No.

BARBS. You will do anyway. Soon. Oh yes you will, Grant, you're going away, remember? Australia, Japan –

GRANT. That was before I met you.

BARBS. Grant, you are a young man. With places to go. I am pushing forty.

GRANT. Thirteen years, Barbs. Look at you! What difference does it make.

BARBS. All the difference in the world.

BRENDAN. All that while we were trying for a baby you were having it off with him? Christ, that makes me feel sick.

DAVIE. You never wanted a baby . . .

BARBS. Neither did you.

GRANT. You were trying to have a baby with that poof while you were so totally paranoid about me being careful?

BARBS. Yes I was. And more than you know. I used my cap as well. Condoms and cap. Belt and braces. Because the last thing I wanted was to trap you, Grant. You have to go . . .

BRENDAN. Well, as it turns out we were wasting our time, Barbara.

I went and got a sperm count. Because it sort of bothered me we'd been trying for a few months and no joy. I know, I know, we said we'd give it the six months, then we'd go for tests together, see if all was well. Because there was things could be done, *assisted* things you'd been reading about in all yon books . . . Well, there was nothing could have been done for you and me, Barbs, because – oh, and this came as big a shock to me as it would to the next man, believe me – I have just about the lowest sperm count they have ever registered. Less than a million per millilitre and zero motility. No chance, Barbs. We'd never – never in a million years – have been parents.

BARBS. I am pregnant.

A silence. BARBS *begins to laugh weirdly. Stops again.*

BARBS. I thought to myself, no, I'll only be late because of . . . Everything. This week of all weeks, eh? I thought don't get all excited. But I just did a pregnancy test. And it was positive. The stick changed colour.

BRENDAN, GRANT *and* DAVIE. Whose baby is it?

BARBS. It is mine!

BRENDAN. Well, I am out of here. Barbs, bye, that is you and me finished.

BRENDAN *walks out the door.*

BARBS. I want you all to go.

GRANT. I'm going nowhere.

DAVIE. Barbs, just you say the word, doll, and I'll stiffen this bastard.

BARBS. Leave me alone, Davie.

DAVIE. I'll stay with you, doll. Long as you need me.

BARBS. Leave me!

He does finally. Walks out the door. Leaving BARBS, ALICE, GRANT.

ALICE. You just couldn't see me happy, could you, without you having to take him away from me?

GRANT. I won't ever leave till you tell me to my face you don't want me.

BARBS. I want my mother!

She breaks down at last. Eventually –

ALICE. Grant, there's tea made. Pour the three of us, c'mon, a wee cup of tea . . .

He doesn't. Folds his arms. Eventually ALICE is forced to go to the tea tray and pour it herself.

ALICE. Aye well, I suppose I'll better be mother . . .

She starts to laugh. Not a particularly merry laugh, but she does find it – literally – absolutely – hysterical.

ALICE. I do not believe I said that! (*Beat.*) *Grand*mother I suppose I should say . . .

ALICE looks up to see GRANT and BARBS in each others arms. He's rocking her, stroking her back, soothing her, holding her.

To herself –

ALICE. Ach well, as they say, you'd think I'd no home to go to, eh? . . . Ah'll better away . . .

ALICE goes to the door.

BARBS. Alice, please don't go. I need you.

BARBS disentangles herself from GRANT's arms.

BARBS. Grant. Darling. It's not yours.

GRANT. But he said –

She pushes him gently away from her with one hand.

BARBS. I am absolutely sure, my darling, this baby isn't yours.

Black.

Music bridge: Annie Lennox: 'No More I Love Yous (Language is Leaving Me . . .)'.

Scene Five

BARBS *alone. zonked out on the sofa. Asleep. She wears a loose almost Greek-looking nightgown and is barefooted. The picture of the classic dreaming girl . . .*

The ghost of SADIE *appears. As a young mother in 1961 or 1962,* SADIE *has a puffball or a pencil skirt, stilettos, big hair and she wheels one of those sixties coach built prams. She crosses the stage simply and exits. Singing 'I love you a bushel and a peck'.*

BARBS *wakes up and joins in '. . . A bushel and a peck and a hug around the neck'. She does not look at* SADIE *but seems to quite simply feel her presence as she passes by.* SADIE *disappears as lights change.*

Standing on the floor is a large plastic bronze coloured bottle. A little larger than a sweetie jar. On the table is a beautiful empty shallow dish. BARBS *opens the jar and solemnly, experimentally, pours some of these, her mother's, ashes into the dish. There is a sifting of fine grey ash, but a few carbon-y coke like black burnt bone lumps too. She goes to touch, curious.*

As she does, The downstairs buzzer goes.

BARBS *jumps. Then slipping her feet into giant silly novelty furry slippers, she goes and answers at the intercom.*

BARBS. Hello? Who is it?

BRENDAN'S VOICE. It's me . . .

BARBS. Brendan? It's late Brendan. But, Yeah. Yeah come on up.

She presses the button then goes back to the table, puts the plastic crematorium jar down behind it. The inside bell goes. She opens the door.

BRENDAN *comes in.*

BRENDAN. Hello Barbs.

BARBS. Hello stranger.

BRENDAN. I met Tiff – first time I've even seen anybody – I bumped into her on Waverly Station and she told me you were moving!

BARBS. – Need a garden. This place is on the market. Offers over a hundred and ninety five would you believe –

BRENDAN. Oh, well I'll speak to my broker right away! (*Beat.*)
I've missed you, Barbara. Very very long time no see, eh?

BARBS. A whole year. You missed my birthday. Bastard. You
missed my big Four O.

BRENDAN. How was that?

BARBS. Very quiet. I was nearly five months pregnant at the time,
so . . .

BRENDAN. How is she?

BARBS. Perfect. It's hard work. She's beautiful.

BRENDAN. Like her Mammy, eh? I, emm, brung her up a wee
lamb.

He produces a soft toy lamb. Small and very sweet.

BRENDAN. Grace, eh?

BARBS. That's right. That's lovely, Brendan. She'll love it. She's
sleeping, but she's due to wake up soon.

BRENDAN. Grace. Imagine.

BARBS. Grace Sarah Kirkwood. After my Mum.

BRENDAN. Was that her name? Sadie?

BARBS. She was Sarah Grace Kirkwood . . .

I couldn't call her Marshall. The baby. I mean, I am stuck with
Davie's name for the duration I suppose, but I couldn't give it
to Grace, could I? So she has my family name. The one I grew
up with. My father's name . . .

BRENDAN. Him that you don't remember?

BARBS. Yeah . . . Davie and I got divorced, by the way.

BRENDAN. How was that?

BARBS. Fine. He came up with a bottle of champagne and two of
milk stout and made Black Velvet which he said was good for
my breastfeeding.

BRENDAN. How's his . . . relationship?

BARBS. Oh . . . (*She makes a so-so gesture with her hand.*) Things
will never be right until when and if the lovely Colette tells her
rich father to fuck off. But, that's between her and Davie . . .

BRENDAN. I broke up with Cammy.

BARBS. Oh, Brendan . . .

She hugs him. They hold a moment.

BRENDAN. A couple of months back. But, och, you know what they say about gay relationships being measured in dog years . . . In that case Cammy and I made it well past the seven year itch stage.

BARBS. Och, Brendan I'm sorry. Was it hellish?

BRENDAN. Pretty bad. But, och, I'm back amongst the walking wounded . . .

BARBS. How is the job?

BRENDAN. That *is* hellish. Plus the commute to Edinburgh is doing my head in. I was thinking of flitting through, but then I thought do I want to live in a gay scene dominated by Q.C.'s and candidates for the new Scottish Parliament . . . ?

BARBS. Wanting to come back to Razor City?

BRENDAN. In a minute. But what would Stefan say?

BARBS. Please. Maternity may have turned my brain to mince, but in Razor City I do still have an equal say. Plus Stefan would be the first to admit we have never found, nor ever will find, a cutter to match you.

You can come back if you'll come with me tomorrow.

BRENDAN. What's tomorrow?

BARBS. Tomorrow is the anniversary of my mother's funeral.

BRENDAN. I remembered, yes. (*Beat.*) It's Mother's Day tomorrow.

BARBS. Yeah, well I'm a mother amn't I? So I can do what I want.

What I was going to do tomorrow, well the weather's been nice, so I thought I'd like to take Grace, she loves it in her backpack, we are going to take my mother's ashes up to the top of this hill – my mother was always talking about this place, my father used to take us there. I don't remember it but I remember my mother talking about it, Mum, Dad, me, our Billy, well he was only a baby, maybe wasn't even born yet. We'd go for picnics and there was a waterfall called the Grey

Mare's Tail. It's south, down the main road, near Moffat, I found it on the map, not far . . .

I want you to come with us. I want us to take Sadie's ashes and let them go. Over the waterfall. Then I want us to have a picnic. Family only. You, me and Grace.

BRENDAN. What can I say?

BARBS. Say yes. Say it!

BRENDAN. Yes.

BARBS. Perfect.

BRENDAN. Speaking of perfect, how's whatsisface? My . . . rival for your affections?

BARBS. Grant? Very good I think. Last I heard was a postcard from Ayers Rock at Christmas. Alice and I got the exact same one.

BRENDAN. Do you miss him?

BARBS. No.(*Beat.*) Definitely not as much as Alice does.

BRENDAN. Did you love him?

BARBS. Oh yes. I did do.

BRENDAN. I solved the mystery.

BARBS. What mystery?

BRENDAN. The . . . paternity. Didn't it worry you?

BARBS. No.

BRENDAN. Christ, that's honest.

BARBS. Brendan, I have, for the last year, had more to bother me than that. Pregnancy. Do you know how you are meant to blossom? Glow? Forget it. I felt like shit the whole time. Physically. Inside myself I never regretted it for a minute.

Giving birth. Agony. I can't tell you. Ask Alice! Alice was my birth partner. She stayed with me. Held my hand. Through absolute bloody agony. Till my nails gouged into her hand, made her bleed. Kept on hanging on.

And Grace . . . Changed everything.

(*Beat.*) Sometimes I even feel as if I can understand my own mother.

BRENDAN (*amazed*). Can you?

BARBS. No. But I miss her.

BRENDAN. The baby is Cammy's. In the matter of her . . . biological paternity.

BARBS. What?

BRENDAN. He switched jars.

BARBS. He what?

BRENDAN. Remember how we used to – then I'd bring it round? He was jealous. He –

BARBS. – Produced his own and switched the jars! That is brilliant. When Ma sent me that strippogram she didn't know it but she was certainly sending me quite a present. Thank you, Sadie . . .

BRENDAN. Can I go through and see her.

BARBS. 'Course you can . . . bring her through, she's due a feed anyway.

BRENDAN takes the lamb and goes off.

BRENDAN (*offstage*). Hello. Hello, darling . . . (*Beat. Then loudly.*) She's gorgeous, Barbsie! Beautiful.

He comes on with a baby of four months wrapped in his arms.

BRENDAN. Hello! Hello, it's your Auntie Brenda, your fairy godmother . . .

BARBS goes to him. They make a beautiful tender family tableau.

BRENDAN. Do you know who she is the spitting image of? Across the eyes?

BARBS. Don't!

BRENDAN. Your mother . . .

They laugh together in sheer joy. It coming streaming out from them, expanding, lifting.

Music: Lou Reed's 'Perfect Day' in the current multi-voiced and soaring BBC version.

End.

A Nick Hern Book

Perfect Days first published in Great Britain as an original paperback in 1998 by Nick Hern Books Limited, 14 Larden Road, London W3 7ST

Second revised edition 1999

Cover image: Siobhan Redmond as Barbs (photo Euan Myles)

Lyrics from the song *If Not You* by Dennis Locorriere on p. 36 copyright © 1998 Screen Gems–EMI Music Inc, Screen Gems–EMI Music Ltd, London WC2H 0EA. Reproduced by permission of IMP Ltd.

Typeset by Country Setting, Kingsdown, Kent CT14 8ES
Printed in England by Cox and Wyman Ltd, Reading, Berks

ISBN 1 85459 437 0

A CIP catalogue record for this book is available from the British Library